Fighting for Your Full Potential

Unleash your Greatness Within & Experience Nothing but Wins!

By Jenise R. McNair

Copyright 2020. Jenise McNair. All right reserved.

This book or parts thereof may not be reproduced in any form, stored in any retrieval system, or transmitted in any form by any means—electronic, mechanical, photocopy, recording, or otherwise—without prior written permission of the publisher, except as provided by United States of America copyright law. For permission requests, write to the publisher, at JeniseMcNair@FreeHerTruths.com at the address below.

Visit the author's website at www.JeniseMcNair.com

Edited and formatted by Andrea McCurry

Cover designed by Monica Stanley

Photographer by Calvin Wade, Jr.

ISBN:978-1-7348331-3-3

Used with permission

Acknowledgements

To God, thank you for continuing to show favor upon me. Thank you for restoring my life and filling my spirit with so much peace, comfort, and joy. Made in the image and likeness of you; thank you for showing me that with you, all things are possible. Forever, I'll give you all the Glory!

To my late mother, My Queen, Joan H. McNair. There isn't a day when I don't think of you. Thank you for being the selfless mother you've been to your family and for teaching what it means to sacrifice for the things we want out of life. I'll forever carry you in my spirit, my mind, and most of all, my heart. I love you with everything in me and I pray that I am making you proud. Love you always and forever, your Baby Girl.

To my three amazing children Jelani, Jaylah, and Jordyn. It is such an honor being your mother. Every day that I wake up, it is imperative that I give you the greatest version of myself. The three of you deserve the best that life has to offer and as your mother, giving you less than that is unacceptable. I continue to set expectations of myself that cause me to grow as an individual so that I can give you all that is needed from me.

When I look at each of you, I can't help but to get excited about your future. The three of you have your own special gifts and I can't wait for you to share them with the world. As you continue to learn and grow, I expect for you all to value your time; take advantage of any opportunity that will allow you to get better. You must always be willing to do the work and show up for yourself every single day.

As I continue to guide and lead you as your mother, I only ask that you seek greatness and unleash the greatness that's inside of you! Embrace your own personal journeys and know all things are possible for those who believe. Thank you for your unconditional love and support as I go after my dreams. You all are my greatest accomplishments! Mommy loves the three of you with my whole heart and everything on the inside of me!

To my brother and my sister, Daniel and Talia. Thank you for being my ride or die. You both play such a significant role in my life. Being the youngest sibling has always been my security. I knew that no matter what, I would always have you to stand on in my time of need. Between the three of us, we have a relationship that can't be broken. I truly cherish that I can call my siblings my best friends. Besides Daddy, you two are the BEST(in my DJ Khaled voice.) Thank you for always loving me and doing your part as my older siblings to always look out for me. Being the youngest is truly something special when you have a big brother and sister like you. I love you two with everything in me. Let's continue to make mom and dad proud! #McNairsForever

Dedication

I dedicate this book to my father, Aaron D. McNair. The wins I have experienced in life, I truly owe them to you. Having you in my corner is nothing but God's reflection of His undying love for me. Your strength and fortitude towards adversity is truly amazing. I can't help but continue to push through life, knowing the adversities you've faced. Your positivity and your faith gave me hope in my toughest times. You made me want to fight for my full potential.

When I look at the woman I've become, I can't help but to be so thankful for the loving and supportive father you have always been to me. You continue to encourage me to accomplish any goals that I set out to achieve. And no matter what my journey may look like ahead, I can always count on your support to see my vision through.

Thank you, Daddy, for being everything I ever need you to be and more. You are an amazing father, a loving Pop-Pop, and such a selfless man. As long as I have breath in my body, I will continue to honor you and do all that I can to add happiness and joy to your life. May God continue to bless you and keep you healthy and happy! I promise to continue to make you proud by evolving and becoming the woman you've raised me to be. Love you, Daddy. I'm forever your Baby Girl!

Preface

Throughout all of my hardships and lessons learned, I've realized that I've become addicted to Winning. Being knocked down so many times and feeling like losing was always going to be part of my life was miserable. When we lose in life, we're left with nothing but a nagging feeling of defeat. Defeat gets under your skin and causes you to question your worthiness and your capability to win. Once you've experienced so many losses in life, you start to see yourself as a loser.

There was a point in my life when I felt like I lost everything and nothing good was ever going to happen to me. I was on a losing streak, for sure. Then one day, I spoke with my dad and he reminded me of the time I almost lost my life. He told me that when I was two years old, I was on the floor of the kitchen while my mother was cooking. My dad decided to walk in the kitchen and saw me turn purple as I struggled, trying to breathe. He ran over to me and realized something was blocking my airway. He stuck his finger down my little throat and pulled a bottle cap out. My mom burst out crying, saying if my dad hadn't come in the kitchen when he did, I would've probably lost my life. I don't know how long the bottle cap was stuck in my throat but I wasn't going out without a fight. I always call my dad my superhero because he really did save my life.

When I think about all the losses I've endured, I tell myself the devil has been after me since I was two years old. But God has a reason for me to be here today. He sent my dad into the kitchen at just the right time so that the devil couldn't take my life. Even after that moment, the devil has been on a warpath, trying to take what he could from me and causing me defeat.

I had to realize that I was the one who had the control to change the narrative of my story when it came to losing. I was only losing because I didn't do what was necessary to win. But since I got a hold of a winning mindset, I've become addicted to winning.

I was able to change the narrative of my story by finally making the decision to choose me. For years, I allowed my own personal truths to drive fear in me instead of faith. I had to dig way down into the depths of who I was. By taking time out to heal and conquer my fears, I started to unleash the Greatness on the inside of me. I thought my personal truths were only setbacks but it turned out that my personal truths were my Greatest Weapon. The power behind your truth is what gives you the confidence to fearlessly go after your Dreams.

Every day when I wake up, I make it my business to be better than who I was yesterday. Every day, I fight to live up to my potential that's on the inside of me. I no longer go down without a fight; I no longer accept losses unless I know that I gave my all.

Most people know they have potential but they don't know how to effectively live up to it. They don't ignite that burning desire that's on the inside of them. You start to tap into your full potential when you make the choice to choose you, to work on you, and to do whatever is necessary to become whoever you desire to be. For every loss you experience in life, there's a journey ahead that leads to nothing but wins. But you only experience those victories when you make a choice to do what's necessary to fight for your potential. Let me be the person to tell you that you *ARE WORTH THE FIGHT!*

Contents

Introduction

1. **Who Are You?**
2. **A Limitless Mind**
3. **Be Hungry**
4. **Non-Negotiable**
5. **Winning Circle**
6. **Learning & Mastery**
7. **UNLEASH**
8. **WINdemic**

About the Author

Introduction

I've always played sports my entire childhood and basketball was the sport I absolutely fell in love with. From the age of nine up until I entered high school, I was always a starting player. I was much taller than everyone else when I was younger so I played center and power forward. By the time I got to high school, everyone seemed to pass me in height and I was no longer considered tall, which meant my position needed to be changed.

My parents sent me to private school because they didn't want me going to the public high school in my neighborhood. They knew what was best for me because I was a child who needed structure, otherwise I probably wouldn't have made it out of high school! At the very beginning of the school year, I sprained my ankle practicing during open gym so I didn't have the opportunity to try out for Varsity basketball. I ended up playing for the Junior Varsity team and I was one of the stars of the team.

In the middle of the season, I was asked to move up to the Varsity team. Of course, I was excited to be on Varsity but little did I know, I wasn't going to get much playing time. In my mind, I didn't understand why the coach took me off Junior Varsity just to sit on the bench for Varsity. But since I was a freshman, I told myself to suck it up and just be thankful to be on Varsity.

My sophomore year came and I still didn't receive much playing time. In high school being 5'5 was no longer tall so I had to start working on playing outside positions. I was always good at rebounding, playing defense, and going hard while I was on the court but I never really developed an offense. As my sophomore year continued, I still wasn't playing much because we had so many talented players on one team. We had a MONSTER SQUAD! As the season came to an end, I felt disappointed that I spent most of it riding the bench.

I loved basketball and I wanted to play. I played for a winning team but I still felt like a complete loser. I knew my game was going to have to get better if I was going to have any chance of playing my junior year. The whole summer, my brother and I did drills daily and shot over the house. I even went to a shooting training camp to work on my jumper. The whole summer, I focused on getting better and developing an offense. And by August, I developed a jumper that was a nothing-but-net jumper!

I went to the gym with my sister-best friends and I told our play Brother how I worked on my game and developed a jumper over the summer. He laughed at me and said, "Who got a jumper? Not you!"

"Yes, I do!" I said.

So, he said, "Okay, lets' play Around the World for money. For every three pointers you make, I'll give you $5."

The first three shots I made, he was in awe. By the time the game was over, he owed me $100! He was so shocked and couldn't believe I shot so well. To this day, he talks about how I hustled him for his money! I tried to tell him!

Well, my junior year came and practice started back up for the new season. In practice, I scored more and consistently shot jumpers. I worked hard over the summer so I could earn some time on the court. When the season started, I did great in practice but I still didn't get any playing time during the games. At this point, I was frustrated and couldn't take it anymore. All I wanted was a fair chance to play but I was still sitting on the bench! The team traveled and beat teams left and right but a part of me still felt like I wasn't contributing to those wins which bothered me.

Everyone on the team was like a sister to me and although I enjoyed my teammates, deep down I was truly unhappy not being able to play. Finally, I had a conversation with my coach and expressed my disappointment in not being able to play. And I'll never forget how he looked at me and said, "Everyone's role on the team isn't to be out on the court. You play a major role on this team. You are the glue that keeps everybody together! Because of your personality, you make people smile and you have a good spirit."

Even though I understood what he was trying to say, that still wasn't good enough for me. My nickname was Wonda Bread! I was always the player that danced, laughed, and got the team hyped up before we went out to play a game. That was the role the coach believed I played for the team. But all my life, I played ball. I was a ball player and I wasn't interested in making people feel good at that time. Nothing would satisfy me but having a chance to play. Because the conversation didn't go the way I wanted, I ended up storming out the gym and QUIT THE TEAM!

I called my mom to pick me up and when I got in the car, I burst out crying, telling her what I did. She knew how much I loved ball so she asked, "What do you want to do?"

"I'm leaving the school altogether," I responded.

It was Junior year and it was halfway through the season. I also had to consider my high-school sweetheart who I had been with since my freshman year. Moving schools also meant leaving behind all my friends and teammates who were like my sisters. Was I really going to leave all of them just for basketball?

In that moment, I had to make a choice: stay at private school and not play basketball, stay on the team and sit on the bench, or leave to fight for my own potential. As hard as that decision was with all the pressure to make a choice that could change my future, I chose me! My boyfriend broke up with me and I cried like a baby but I had to do what was best for me.

As I pulled up to my neighborhood school, my mom said to me, "Cut up in here if you want to, but you'll be right back at the private school." When I walked in the office, I immediately saw my sister- best friends who were also transferring to the school to play ball. This simultaneous transfer wasn't planned; we didn't know until we saw each other. At that moment, I knew I made the right decision. My choice was Divine!

Our new coach told the local newspaper that he just received three Christmas gifts! The coach truly saw greatness in me from the first time we met. He saw me as someone valuable to his team and I didn't take for granted. *One man's trash is another man's treasure!* Not only did I want to prove to him right, I wanted to prove to myself that I was capable of living up to my full potential on the basketball court. During that season I scored and shot three-pointers like never before.

I saw my old coach at a tournament and he asked, "Where did all that scoring come from?"

I responded, "You never gave me a chance."

He hugged me and said, "I'm Sorry!" There was no love lost and to this day, I still love him! I was grateful and I respected him for being able to apologize to me. His apology meant more to me than anything. During my senior year, I led the county in three pointers and averaged 15 points a game. My one decision to choose to live up to my potential was a defining moment for me. I felt like I was a loser but it was up to me to change the narrative of my story and I did!

I think we can all agree that feeling like a loser, in some form or capacity, isn't a good feeling. We have all suffered from the pressures of life when it comes down to trying to get ahead. We spend too much time investing in people and material things that can't help us get ahead and we don't put enough time into ourselves and our potential. We all have goals and dreams that we one day would like to see manifested. But the problem is, many of us aren't willing to do the work. For some odd reason, we think the life that we desire to have is just going to magically fall into our laps. We want a good life but we aren't making an effort towards having the life we desire. If everyone made a choice to fight for their full potential as if their lives were on the line, how many happy, successful people would we have in the world today?

As humans, it's normal to be our own worst critics. Our past traumas, careless mistakes, and painful truths cause us to think we aren't capable of living up to our fullest potential.

We look at the next person and compare our lives with theirs. Negative thoughts of oneself can't produce greatness. They won't produce anything but continual losses that we try to blame on others.

Winning is a mindset! There's no secret to winning, you just have to believe that you are capable of winning in every area of your life. You gain a winning mindset by choosing to believe in yourself and being positive, even in the most difficult times. In order to live the life we've always imagined living, we must be willing to do whatever it takes to succeed. Winning doesn't happen by some sort of magic that allows us to live happily ever after! Winning requires Perseverance, Commitment, and Determination.

Can you think of a time when you watched a basketball or football team win a championship by doing absolutely nothing? Unfortunately, most teams lose because they didn't do enough. That's how life is; we lose because we aren't doing enough! We also lose by making choices that aren't best for us and by being consumed with the opinions of others.

Think about where you are today in your life and imagine where you would like to be. Can you honestly say you have done all that is necessary to take you where you want to be in life? Have you worked on yourself internally each day or worked on your goals to make your dreams a reality?

It's challenging to have difficult conversations with other people but it's even more challenging to have difficult conversations with yourself. It's a harsh reality when you have to accept the truth and you wonder why your life isn't going as planned. You must be able to honestly look at yourself in the mirror and say, "It's because I'm not doing enough!" Having honest conversations like that with yourself is the first step to changing the narrative of your story.

How are you going to change for the better when you can't even identify the changes that need to be made? If you feed yourself lies, you'll continue to live in a false existence but if you feed yourself the truth, you'll do whatever is necessary to make your dreams a reality. How can you move forward in life if you aren't able to identify what's holding you back? It's so important that we evaluate who we are as an individual, the good, the bad, and the ugly. Becoming the person you desire in life is a process; it's a journey that never ends. You never stop learning so you are always evolving into someone better.

The better you know and accept yourself, the better prepared you will be for challenges at the higher level.
—Mike Williams

We become the person we desire to be through hardship, failures, and adversities. Those elements of life are not supposed to break us; they are supposed to build us up. We need to take every experience and apply it to our lives as we move forward, learning what's right, what's wrong, what's good, and what's bad for us. We are able to identify those different elements by the experiences we have gone through. Then we can take those learned lessons and apply them to our everyday lives.

What good is a mistake if we don't learn from that error? Our mistakes aren't bad. They only become detrimental when we choose to make the same mistake over and over again. Learning from your flaws or setbacks plays a huge role in your growth as an individual and determines your level of success.

Reaching the highest level of your potential is really based off the work you are willing to put into yourself. You will always have to work towards reaching the highest level of your potential because your potential has no limits. There should never be a day where you don't take the time to work on you! You must work on different elements that will cause you to become a better version of yourself. Challenging and pushing yourself to consistently improve will stimulate your mind and cause you to grow.

We often put a lot of time and energy into everyone else but ourselves. In order to take yourself to the next level, you have to identify what adds value to your life and what doesn't. You have to be willing to make tough decisions even if it involves telling someone 'no' or letting someone go. If you have a heart and you truly care about your loved ones, it is easy to stretch yourself thin, trying to care for them. Adding value to other people's lives while failing to add value to your own life will leave you feeling empty.

For so long I used to say, "I'm such a good person. I'm always going out of my way to make sure everyone is happy." Yet, difficult circumstances continued to happen to me. On my journey to become the greatest version of myself, I had to realize I was giving other people what I should've been offering to myself first. There's nothing wrong with wanting to be there for other people but how can you truly be available to others if you can't even help yourself first? When you fill your cup up and it starts to overflow, the overflow is what you take to share with others. Continue to keep yourself full and your cup will overflow for others in need.

When I hit rock bottom in my own life, I owed it to myself to do whatever was necessary to beat the odds that were set against me. I had to accept accountability and ownership over my life. It was important for me to fight to reach my own potential and see what I was really made of. In order to get a better life, I had to be willing to do whatever was necessary to become a better person. I had to have that difficult conversation with myself and accept that I hit rock bottom because *"I wasn't doing enough."*

Doing the bare minimum was not going to change the narrative of my story. Doing the bare minimum meant I wasn't caring for myself in various areas of my life, including financially, physically, or emotionally. I realized doing the bare minimum, was not going to give me the life that I desired for my kids and myself. I understood that if I wanted a better life and I truly wanted to live up to my full potential, I was going to have to *fight for it!*

The difference between ordinary and extraordinary

is that little extra.

—Jimmy Johnson

It doesn't matter what you've been through, what people said you couldn't do, or what you wish you had known. What matters the most is making the commitment to fight for your own potential. Tell yourself that doing the bare minimum is no longer acceptable. You are worth all the time, the energy, the dedication, and the effort that it takes to become the person God called you to be. You have all the power and ability to succeed and that should give you a sense of security, knowing nothing can hold you back from making your dreams a reality! Being good just isn't good enough; so why not be *GREAT!*

When you fight for your full potential, that's when you make the impossible possible!

Who Are You?

If you are always trying to be normal you will never know how amazing you can be.

— Maya Angelou

If someone asked you right now, "Who are you?" what would your response be? You would be surprised at how many people can't honestly answer that question. So many people struggle with not knowing who they are or what they want out of life.

We aren't meant to live forever but do you aspire to leave a legacy behind you that will continue to live on? What do you want to be known for? Unfortunately, we can't live up to our full potential without knowing who we are first. We can't live up to our full potential without owning, walking, and embracing our personal truths. I am a firm believer that walking in truth will give you the freedom to soar without any restrictions to confine you.

For so long I struggled with my own identity, trying to run from past traumas that I thought determined who I was as a person. I put limitations on my potential, thinking that my past decided who I could be. I allowed my former circumstances to make me question the greatness that God put inside of me. If we don't know who we are, then we only allow the world and the opinion of others to define who we are.

It's not easy trying to overcome circumstances in your life that make you feel stuck and lost. But what I do know is, when you walk in your truth, you can overcome anything that you put your mind to and you can become the person you desire to be in life, no matter what you've gone through.

Who are you? It's a simple question that we should know about ourselves. You are whatever you believe you are and you are whoever you say you are. The only limitations we have are the ones we place on ourselves. It's important for us to understand that our words hold so much power. Who we are starts with what we think and say about ourselves. We must speak life and not death.

Words of affirmation play a major role in filling our spirits with positivity and hope. Learn to look in the mirror every day, saying to yourself, "I am great! I am a Warrior. My past doesn't define me. I am whoever I say I am and I am capable of becoming the person I desire to be in life." Who are you? No one will ever understand you more than you understand yourself.

Before I could become who I desired to be in life, I had to understand that my past doesn't define me. It was hard to drown out what I had become based off the painful truths I had to overcome in my life. I tried to deny that I was sexually abused as a child, became a mom at the age of 19, dropped out of college, allowed myself to be in an abusive relationship, and then had to apply for public assistance to take care of my kids. It was hard telling myself that I wasn't a failure when my life seemed to display it was. "Who am I?" was an easy question to ask but my response at that point was, "I'm a complete failure."

Growing up, I was the youngest of my two siblings and I didn't want to do everything that they were interested in. They both went to college and graduated with degrees. School wasn't my favorite. I always made the honor roll in elementary and middle school but I went to a private school for the first three years of high school. It was a great school yet making the honor roll was tough for me. I'm old enough now to understand that I could've made honor roll in high school but I didn't apply myself to do what was necessary at the time. You always hear the saying, "I wish I knew back then what I know now." I would've definitely worked harder in high school.

Although my siblings went to college, I knew I wanted to do things a little differently. I enjoyed doing hair growing up and honestly had a passion for it at a young age. My dad used to fuss at me when he came home from work and saw me in the bathroom doing my hair. He used to say, "You in the mirror doing your hair but you need to be in them books and studying."

I responded, laughing, "I have to do my hair for school, Daddy." He got so mad as I stood in the mirror for hours, so dedicated to my hair. He wished I had the same dedication when it came to my schoolwork.

Now that I'm older I definitely agree with him. Being more dedicated to my schoolwork would've allowed me to go to college for free. But in high school, I only did enough to get by so I could be eligible to play basketball, which was my main hobby in high school, along with styling hair. My senior year, I had some colleges interested in me going to their program to play ball. My SAT score was decent but my 2.9 GPA wasn't enough to get by for college ball. Elizabeth City State University and George Mason University were interested in my basketball talents but because of my grades I would've had to redshirt and sit out my first year. Because I was young, I allowed my pride and my ego to make the decision for me, so I passed up on both offers.

Looking back now, I wish I would've taken advantage of the opportunity to be able to go to school for free. Once I declined those two offers, I told my father I wanted to go to hair school instead. After I finished cosmetology school, I could then enroll in college afterwards. I wanted to get my cosmetology license then go to a four-year college so that while I was in college, I could work and make money.

My mom wanted me to go straight to college but my dad saw my vision. He understood that I was my own person and knew I had a gift with hair. He always told me and still does, "Just make sure you have a game plan." He knew it was important for me to figure out what I wanted and to have a clear understanding and a game plan of how to get there. My dad wasn't hung up on me going to college first because my mom went to work for the government straight out of high school since my grandma couldn't afford to send her to college. My dad, however, graduated from college and got a government job as well. Believe it or not, my mom made more money than my dad and he was the one with the college degree. So, my dad always understood that just because you went to college didn't mean you would make a lot of money.

Although I knew I would be compared to my siblings, I still went through with my decision to go to cosmetology school first. After I earned my license, I enrolled in college for my business degree. I wasn't able to finish college because I ended up getting pregnant. Ultimately, my plan still worked for me because with my license, I was able to support my son and me. If I had chosen to go to college first, I would not have had a marketable skill when I had to drop out.

It's important that we understand who we are! We can't make decisions in life based off what someone else thinks about us or those who try to tell us who we are. God created each one of us in the image and likeness of Him but we are also created uniquely in our own way. Our travels in life are not supposed to look like someone else's journey. We have to be able to embrace our own personal expedition and evolve into the person we are destined to be. You are different from the next person for a reason. Only you are able to offer what you are meant to give to the world.

Even if you are at a place in your life where you aren't really certain of who you are, just ask yourself that question and focus on who you would like to become. I believe we have the power and the ability to create the life we desire to live. We are able to create the person we desire to be. In my first book, *Potential of a Man vs. Truth,* I explained how I lost my identity by putting all my energy and time into a man and a toxic relationship. Yet, I rebuilt myself and became a better and even stronger person by walking and embracing my personal truth.

Every day, I worked towards becoming the person I desired to be. I embraced my journey of hardships, understanding that I had the power and the ability to change the narrative of my story. Every day, I made a choice to do something productive that contributed to my quest to become the person I said I wanted to be. I told myself I wanted to become a Best-Selling author and I did. I told myself I wanted to become a Marathoner and I did - seven times. I said I wanted to travel the world and experience different cultures, traveling at least three times a year, and I did.

Becoming who you desire to be in life is an ongoing process. It's a process that allows you to enjoy the journey as you evolve and become. Every day, you should only compete against yourself and try to be better than who you were yesterday.

Knowing who you are, or at least who you want to be, allows you to declare and decree power, love, and self-control over your life. When you don't know who you are or who you want to be, you allow others to fill your spirit with lies of who they say you are. Then you are susceptible to actually believing those lies. Les Brown, one of the greatest motivational speakers of all time says, "Someone's opinion of you doesn't have to become your reality." Understand that you define who you are, no matter what you've had to endure in your life.

Our past plays a big part of how we see ourselves in the mirror. Our traumas, failures, hardships, and painful truths can cause us to only see the negative elements of what we've encountered in life. We think and feel that we are nothing but our mistakes; we allow our past to get the best of us. We believe we aren't capable of going after all of our dreams and aspirations.

It's so important to be set free from the painful truths that keep us held captive. We often allow those negative truths and experiences to control our lives and our every move. We must understand that no matter what we've been through in life, we have the power and the ability to change the narrative of our story.

I had to get to a place in my life where I was able to acknowledge my behavior and my poor decisions. I had to take ownership and accountability over my life. How many times have we heard the saying "It's not how you start the race that matters but instead it's how you finish." You are not your mistakes in life. Our mistakes are a part of the process of learning and evolving into the people we were all destined to be.

We look at hardships in such a negative way when we should really always view life with a positive eye. One of the greatest lessons I've learned is to only focus on what I can change and just pray about what I can't fix at the moment. That mindset truly reformed my life for the better and it's what I continue to apply in every aspect of my life. I focus on only what I can change.

Even at the worst time in my life, I had to ask myself, "Who am I?" Back then, I was a woman who was emotionally broken, a woman searching for healing by trying to help others, a woman who stretched herself so thin carrying everybody else's burdens. I was a woman with so much potential but I always made a choice to fight for other people's potential instead. Blood, sweat, and tears were spent trying to make everyone else happy but myself.

There will come a time in your life when, in order to change the narrative of your story, you must be willing to CHOOSE YOU! I had to stop focusing on the failures of who I *seemed* to be at the time and started focusing on who I *wanted* to be. I had to ask myself, "Are you finally ready to choose you for once?" Go after all your dreams and aspirations and never look back!

Until you learn how to depart from your past, you'll never know what it is like to arrive. Stop beating yourself down; what's done is done. You are bigger than your circumstances. You are greater than any obstacle that challenges you at the moment. Life is going to happen. Mistakes are going to be made. But change is only possible when you are willing to put in the work.

When the chips were down for me, I made a vow to myself to do whatever was necessary to become the person I desired to be. I chose to fully take control over my life and no longer let my past limit me. I started to speak life instead of death. I spoke positive affirmations daily instead of beating myself down because of past decisions. I called things into my life that did not exist as though they were already in my life. I started to think about all the goals that I wanted to attain but I knew I couldn't accomplish anything without working on me from the inside out.

Self-development will allow you to reassess the areas that you need to work on. Self-Development is the necessary foundation for your dreams to become a firm reality. I believe that your success is built on the foundation of who you are.

I started to do the impossible when I started believing in myself. Who are you, Jenise? I am everything I desire to be and more. To the world, I was a college dropout but I became a best-selling author anyway! To the world, I was a single mother of three on public assistance but I became a mother of three making six figures and giving my children a life that they deserve. To the world, I was miserable, overweight, and never took the time to focus on me but I became a seven-time marathoner who is now healed and set free.

You aren't your mistakes, poor decisions, or painful truths in life. You are a champion, a survivor, a warrior, a child of the Most High, and most of all, a person who was born to achieve great accomplishments in life.

The Covid-19 pandemic of 2020 was life-changing for everyone. A lot of financial lessons were taught and many people were forced to re-evaluate their lives. Fifty million Americans lost their jobs and were left with no income. I was one of those who was affected by the pandemic and lost my job. But instead of looking at that situation in a negative way, I continued to work on me and came up with a different game plan that set my family and me up for success. I didn't focus on what I couldn't change, which was the pandemic and the loss of my job. But what I could change was making sure I continued to push forward, focusing on me and my own business. Although I lost my job during the pandemic, I also became a best-selling author. I didn't allow what was going on around me to take me off my course.

Just like any other storm of life, even the pandemic shall pass. Because of my mindset, I was able to put myself in the position where I had multiple opportunities to make my dreams come true. Although there was a pandemic going on, I knew that I had to stay focused and use my available time wisely. I chose to write another best-selling book to show people how they can live up to their full potential. That achievement was only possible because I chose to keep going, despite what was happening around me. I couldn't focus on the pandemic; I had to only focus on what I could change and that was who I wanted to become.

So again, I ask you, *"Who Are You?"* Take your answer and Internalize it, Visualize it, until you Materialize it! You must know who you are before you can accomplish any goals or dreams you have. Knowing who you are will give you the confidence to do whatever is necessary. Take the steps and achieve your best.

Reflect & Refocus Key Points:

- Ask yourself, Do I know who I am? Do I know who I want to become?
- Also ask: Am I allowing my past or others to determine my future?
- Believing in yourself requires self-development. Work on the areas of your life that you can reform and improve.
- Your success is built on the foundation of who you are.
- Embrace and understand that your journey won't look like the next person's.
- Most of all, accept and own your personal truths.

So again, I ask you, *"Who Are You?"* We don't have the power to go back in life and change our past but we do have the power and ability to move forward and create the future we desire to have.

When you fight for your full potential, that's when you make the impossible possible!

A Limitless Mind

*Being challenged in life is inevitable
but being defeated is optional.*

— Roger Crawford

How many times have you heard someone say, "I wish what I know now, I knew back then?" When I was younger, I didn't know that my thoughts held so much power. How we choose to think can make the difference in the outcome in our circumstances. Our mind is such a powerful tool that we often misuse. Most of our battles in life truly start in our minds. Before we even make a decision, we usually go back and forth in our minds on what we should or shouldn't do. This indecision may affect our ability to achieve positive results. Negative thinking results in a negative outcome and positive thinking results in a more positive outcome.

Unleashing the greatness inside of us truly starts in our minds. When you can break your mental barrier, that's when you start seeing yourself doing the impossible. Your dreams only seem too Big because you haven't allowed your mind to imagine the possibilities of that dream.

God gave us a mind so we can visualize whatever we want. We can see so clearly in our imagination, down to the smallest detail. Our minds contain the virtual tools that allow us to see our Dreams before they manifest into our reality. We have the ability to create the life we desire to have and we are able to experience that life in our minds first through our imagination.

How do we allow each and every day to go by without utilizing and taking advantage of our minds? Most of the time, we allow what we see to determine how we should think. When we are faced with a negative obstacle, it's natural for us to have negative feelings towards that circumstance. Why do we take our minds for granted, not understanding or appreciating the advantages God has given us? Perhaps we don't fully understand the power behind our thinking. The only way to realize the power of the mind is to make the decision to change how we think.

I often visualize myself standing in front of thousands of people, sharing my story and inspiring others to fight for their potential. I clearly hear the crowd clapping and getting excited as I tell them, "You hold the power to create whatever life you desire to have. There isn't anything anyone can do to stop you!"

I also visualize myself sitting in a chair next to one of the best movie producers in the industry, as I help him co-produce a movie based off my best-selling book, *Potential of a Man vs. Truth*. I have images in my mind about having my movie produced and shown on OWN (Oprah Winfrey Network) or Netflix. Maybe even having the first movie produced by Tyler Perry that isn't based on his own material. I allow my mind to take me places in the natural. I think about what I want for myself then I play those desires out in my mind.

Running my first marathon was the start of truly believing all things are possible when you believe. In the beginning, trying to mentally wrap my head around running 26.2 miles was admittedly very overwhelming. Focusing on where I was the moment, having never run more than two miles and being completely out of shape, made that goal seem almost impossible to accomplish. But when I made the decision to at least start, I allowed for myself to just focus on the process of training, one day at a time. I didn't dwell on running the 26.2 miles very often. I just focused on the steps in my training that were going to get me across the finish line. Running my first marathon showed me how the fear in our minds holds us back but how taking action causes us to excel forward. Running that marathon was the defining moment in my life that showed me anything is possible to those who believe.

Most of the time, we talk ourselves out of doing something just because we believe it's too hard to accomplish. Before we ever say yes or no out loud, we have already made a decision in our minds first. That internal subconscious decision affects our results because the body follows the mind. We only take action on what our minds have agreed on first. If our first thought is that we can't, then the end results will follow that thinking. We have to understand that winning in life starts with seeing ourselves as winners in our minds first.

We are only bigger than our circumstances when we *believe* we are bigger than our circumstances. You have to be grounded mentally. If your emotions and mental stability is all over the place then your life will mirror just that!

Feeling defeated is natural but telling yourself you are defeated is a choice. You have to make a choice about accepting defeat when adversity is present. It is so easy to fall into this practice because we make most of our decisions based on how we feel. When we are controlled by our emotions, we allow fear and doubt to make us feel we aren't capable of achieving a goal. But when we make a choice to reject defeat, no matter what obstacle we face, then we take control of the situation, despite how we might feel.

Words of affirmation will fuel the mind with what it needs to believe to achieve a goal that you may feel is impossible. Remind yourself every day, "I am a conqueror. I am not my mistakes. I am worthy. I am valuable. I am strong. I am capable and I am great." The more you say these words, the more you will believe them and not just believe them, but you will also become them! Words of affirmation build self-confidence and they allow you to hold yourself to a higher standard.

I had to see myself as a best-selling author before I became one physically. I had to see myself as a marathoner before I became one in reality. I had to see myself visiting South Africa and Egypt before I actually visited them in person. Every choice starts in our mind and we must stop limiting ourselves by putting restrictions on our imaginations when it pertains to our dreams. Your dreams should be so BIG that when you say them out loud, others look at you like you are crazy!

When I told my family I was writing a book, they all were like, "Oh really?" and didn't' believe I would follow through. As I went through the process of writing, editing, and designing the book cover, their reaction towards my dream started to change. It wasn't that they didn't think I could write a book. It was that they believed that everything I had going on in my life made that dream impossible.

I still remember vividly the day I launched my book. I checked the status on Amazon and saw the Best-Seller ribbon on my book. I started jumping up and down screaming, "OMG! I DID IT I DID IT!" My kids came running downstairs to see what was going on as I fell on the couch, shedding tears of joy! It was the same joy I experienced when I crossed the finish line after running my first Marathon.

With everything I had up against me, working three jobs just to make ends meet, feeling drained from the daily tasks of being a single mom of three, training for a marathon for my mental and physical health, and dealing with the challenges of healing from past traumas, I had to learn how to embrace myself and walk in my personal truths. I continued to push forward and fight for my potential. Most importantly, I continued to believe and have faith in myself, despite what was going on in my life at the moment.

I decided in my mind that I was going to become a best-selling author. I told myself anything less than that wasn't going to be enough. It literally took me six years to complete my first book. With all the challenges and obstacles that I faced, some days felt like I was never going to finish. But I knew I had to keep writing, even if it was only a page or a paragraph each day.

When I started writing my book, I knew it was important for me to finish. I couldn't focus on the fact that while writing, I barely had enough money to feed my kids. I was overwhelmed and weary from all that I had on my plate as a single mom, trying to give my children the life I knew they deserved. But in my mind, I told myself I was a warrior, a survivor, and more than a conqueror. I owed it to myself and to my children to keep my dreams alive no matter what obstacles I faced.

We must understand the sky isn't the limit; it's just a checkpoint. Our minds are so limitless, they can take us places we've always wanted to go. What stops you from executing your goals is that you tell yourself you can't do it! Once you tell yourself you can't do it, that's when the mind shuts down. You allow fear to keep you from what's yours. It's simple to go after goals and dreams that seem easy to obtain. You give yourself a sense of security when you mentally feel capable of accomplishing a goal. Bigger goals and bigger dreams simply mean more work and dedication. Changing your mindset and believing in yourself will give you the sense of security you need to accomplish larger goals. Don't you think your dreams are worth going the extra mile? Yes, because you are worth going the *Extra Mile!*

How we choose to think has a lot to do with our own personal development. Before we can focus on our goals and our dreams, it's important to work on who we are internally. Once I took the time out to work on me and my shortcomings, I started to experience nothing but wins. Before the sun started to shine and the rainbow came out, I had to learn how to create happiness for myself in the midst of the storm. I gave myself my very own intervention; I accepted accountability for the choices I made and no longer made excuses for myself. I knew in order for me to experience a better life for me and my children, I had to change my thinking.

I have always been a very positive person, even though I had to deal with some painful truths that I tried to run from. I will agree that it is very difficult being positive about situations that aren't a reality in your life at the moment. Having a positive mindset in the midst of adversity is what changed my life for the better. One of my favorite quotes by Martin Luther King, Jr. is, "The ultimate measure of a man is not where he stands in moments of comfort and convenience, but where he stands at times of challenge and controversy." I was able to maintain a positive mindset because I made the choice to not allow my current circumstances to get in the way of where I wanted to go. Even in my unfortunate situations, I told myself to only focus on the good that I could take away from them. I vowed to always have a positive attitude, no matter what obstacles I faced.

We can't allow our circumstance to change who we are. Instead we have the power to change our circumstances because of who we are. In order to maintain a positive mindset:

1. Make a choice to remain positive no matter what is in front you.
2. Only focus on what you can change.
3. Try to find the good that is in every unfortunate situation.

These are the steps that I take every day in order to maintain a positive mindset, no matter what circumstances I face. The power of positivity and what it can do in your life is worth you trying.

Most people who experience hardships are only consumed with the problem rather than focusing on finding a solution. In this imperfect world that we live in, you have to learn and know how to adapt without making that change a negative aspect. Bending doesn't always feel good because it can be very uncomfortable. We give up in life or complain about our problems because they take us out of our comfort zone. But challenges bring forth change.

Bending and adapting are good for you because they allow you to always be in control of any situation. When you are able to bend, you have a full understanding that your agenda may not always go as planned and that's okay. Learning to adapt will allow you to always move forward, despite any roadblocks that you find ahead. For example, when there is construction taking place on a route that you normally travel, there is always a detour that will eventually take you in the direction you need to go. And that's exactly how we should operate when we face obstacles; just adapt and find another way! If you aren't open to change, then you will subject yourself to stagnating and remaining stuck in your situation. Change is good because it opens up doors of opportunity in every aspect of your life.

If you look at your circumstances with a positive perspective, you allow yourself to always be in control. Being positive is a choice that we all can make in life. If you are used to being a pessimist, finding a more positive view will take time, consistency and effort, just like any other habit you want to change. Nothing happens overnight and everything we do in life has a process. But you have to be willing to embrace the process and grow while going through it. In order to develop a positive mindset, you must make a choice that being positive is something you will do, no matter what you are faced with. No one said this process will be easy but it will definitely be worth it.

I truly believe there's good in every unfortunate circumstance. In every situation, there's an opportunity to gain wisdom, to grow, and to find an opportunity to help someone else. When we think negatively, we lose all control over the situation and we allow the circumstance to get the best of us.

Our minds are the gateway to prosperity. Tyler Perry didn't allow his circumstances to dictate the future he wanted to create for himself. Being poor and homeless didn't stop him from seeing his vision through. His circumstances only fueled that burning desire inside of him to win by overcoming and going after his dreams. Being a black man in American today, unfortunately, isn't an easy task but his hunger to become great outweighed the obstacles that were placed in front of him. Today, Tyler Perry is worth a billion dollars and built a movie studio on 330 acres with his own airport terminal and strip mall in Atlanta, Georgia. What makes this accomplishment so amazing is that he envisioned this studio and everything he wanted while he was homeless and living out of his car.

This movie studio is new to us but it's old for Tyler Perry because his vision started a long time ago. He became a billionaire. He became the first black owner of his own movie studio. He allowed his thoughts to create a vision that no man could keep him from. He allowed his mind to be the gateway to his prosperity. He didn't allow his circumstances to define him. He understood that what he wanted was going to take a lot of effort, consistency, and hard work.

Despite his circumstances and obstacles, Tyler Perry had a winning mindset. And in order to have a winning mindset, you *MUST* be positive, no matter what! Although, his circumstances may have made him feel like he was losing, he allowed his vision and his dreams to keep pushing him forward. The body can't go where the mind has not already been. Tyler Perry saw himself as Winner and became one! His hardships allowed him to develop *Mental Resilience!*

When you change your mindset, it will truly change your life for the better. You have to think BIG in order to accomplish BIG dreams. Our minds are limitless, and there's nothing too big for the mind. I agree that accomplishing your big dreams can seem overwhelming but that's only because you are trying to accomplish those big dreams overnight. Small victories turn into Big Wins! You must turn your Big Dream into small stepping stones. Every day you should work towards the next stepping stone and celebrate each victory along the way.

You must understand that Big Dreams happen when you choose to put in the work. The harder you work, the faster you accomplish your Big Dreams. We should never settle for only what's expected but instead, we must aim for what's beyond expected. When I was training for my Marathon, not only did I make sure I ran every day but I also challenged myself to eat healthier. I challenged myself to go above and beyond my physical training, giving up what I wanted for what I needed instead.

In order to develop that limitless mind, you must start being mindful of the tasks you do and of the words you speak each day. What we believe and what we say truly holds power and determines the results in your life. When you keep telling yourself that you can't do something, you start to believe that you really can't so you don't even make the effort to try. But when you call yourself a winner and you say to yourself that you are great, you start to believe what you tell yourself.

You must feed your spirit with positivity and encouragement. You must mentally prepare yourself to do what the next person may not be willing to do. What is "going too far" when you are fighting to reach your full potential and going after your dreams? Nothing! Your limitless mindset will allow you to develop mental toughness and mental resilience.

Mental toughness will allow you to persevere through all the challenges that are set in front of you. You fall and you get back up; you fall again and you get back up! You can't allow circumstances to hold you back. Instead, accept that obstacles are going to take place and make the decision to keep moving forward anyway.

*Great things come from hard work and perseverance.
No Excuses!*

—Kobe Bryant

When you mentally tell yourself that you have to keep pushing forward, no matter what, that is what you will do! You push forward with only one goal in mind: that you will accomplish your Dreams. Until you make your dreams happen, the work doesn't stop, even when you are faced with challenges. Once you make up your mind, there shouldn't be any obstacles or person alive that stops you from Winning.

Eric Thomas, an incredible motivational speaker says, **"Winners Win!" Don't ever stop working until you Win!** Winning is a mindset. It is a passion that burns inside you! It fuels you, motivates you, captivates you, and pushes you past the limitations the world tries to set for you! Change your thinking and it will change your life forever.

Your mind is limitless so there should never be a limit on the Dreams that you are capable of having. You have all the power and the ability to make any dream come true. The only person who can stop you from experiencing nothing but wins is you!

Reflect & Refocus Key Points:
- A limitless mind allows you to Dream Big
- If your Dream doesn't scare you, then it's not Big enough
- Make a choice to be positive.
- Mental Toughness and Resilience will push you forward, no matter what you face.
- Small Victories turn into Big Wins
- Celebrate your small wins along the way
- Winners Win so only recognize yourself as just that; a Winner!

Allow your limitless mind to take you places that you envision yourself going. Our mind is truly the gateway to prosperity. Motivational speaker and author Les Brown said, "There are three types of people, millionaires, billionaires, and witnesses." How you see yourself is what you will become in life. I don't know about you, but I've done enough witnessing and it's time for a change! I always refer to myself as a millionaire. Don't limit yourself! You have something to give to the world. Receive it. Believe it. Then give it!

When you fight for your full potential, that's when you make the impossible possible!

Be Hungry

Hunger is the driving force behind personal achievement
—Les Brown

Some studies show that only one percent of people will achieve the success they dream of. Studies also report that only two percent of people who write books actually publish them and only five percent of people who train for marathons complete them. Every chance I get, I do all that I can to beat the odds that are set against me.

Seven years ago, when I thought about how much time I wasted feeling sorry for myself and allowing life to get the best of me, I made up my mind that I was going to persevere and go after all of my dreams. I was no longer going to use the excuse that I was a single mother of three or that it was too late for me to succeed and that I should just let my dreams go. I looked at myself in the mirror and vowed that I was going to fight for my potential. I vowed that I was going to be the example for my children to go after the impossible and make it possible. I owed it to myself to take advantage of the years that I had ahead of me and become the greatest version of myself.

When I think about all the time that I wasted before that decision, when I wasn't focused on me, it makes me so angry. I can't help but think about how much further in life I could've been had I taken advantage of the time that was available for me to work on myself, yet I chose not to. The devil took a lot from me and I wasted years feeling sorry for myself. When I finally stopped focusing on being the "victim," and got hungry to win, that's when I started experiencing victories.

I've become so Hungry, that I go after all of my goals and dreams with dedication and a burning desire to win on the inside. Being hungry means I will use any means possible to go after all of my dreams and aspirations, no matter the odds that are set against me. I refuse to let people, unfortunate circumstances, or hardships hold me back!

Previously, all of my setbacks in life made me feel defeated and like a complete failure. Now, I recognize that those setbacks in life weren't misfortunes; they were just eye openers. They allowed me to look at life through a different set of lenses and see more positively. Changing my mindset to always think the best has caused me to Win more than ever before. Now, all I want to do is win! I'm honestly addicted to winning.

In order to win in every aspect of your life, you must be willing to work on every area of your life. Every year, I am committed to running a marathon. This decision helps me to stay strong mentally and physically. Marathons challenge me, which in turn helps me deal with the obstacles that take place on any given day. Marathons remind me to always stay the course and keep pushing ahead, no matter how I feel. Training isn't always easy but what I gain in the end makes training all worth it! In 2020, because of the global pandemic, my marathons were canceled. I normally run just one marathon a year but I wanted to challenge myself and do two that year. Well, when I found out that both of my marathons were canceled in person, I made a choice that I was going to run 26.2 miles anyway. Twice.

I'm not going to lie and say I wasn't disappointed but I knew training for marathons is much bigger than receiving a medal. Experiencing 100,000 spectators cheering for me, having my family there to support me, and crossing the finish line to receive a medal is an amazing event. But those pleasures are all bells and whistles when it comes to a marathon. The process of training is what I look forward to the most. The person I work so hard to become during the process of training is what I value the most. This undertaking is so important to me because it is in the midst of the process where you evolve. The process is where you dig deep within to conquer any doubts you may have when it comes to accomplishing your goal.

When I train for marathons, I am forced to push myself past the restrictions I mentally set, allowing me to break my mental barriers. While running, I am often tested and challenged to show up for myself by giving all that I have and doing whatever it takes to accomplish the task ahead of me. What I discovered most about myself during my training seasons is my ability to become better every year. Each time, I witness how much I've grown from the year before and I get so excited about my next growth spurt. It's like a kid looking in the mirror and witnessing how much taller they are than before. Growth is a huge motivator for me and I truly enjoy the process of growing and evolving when I train. My goal isn't to run for a medal; my goal every year is to run to get better.

During the 2020 training season, I did something I never thought I could do. I normally work out during the off-season so I won't gain any weight but I don't go as hard as I do during the on-seasons. I typically go to the gym and run three to five miles on the treadmill, four times a week. But I released my first book early in the year and became a Bestselling Author. Let's just say I celebrated every chance I got, eating out, sipping wine, and enjoying that Big Accomplishment! I'm going to be honest, I was not focused on staying in shape or watching what I was eating and I paid for it! Getting in shape seems to take forever but getting out of shape seems like it happens overnight! The pandemic definitely played a part as well since gyms closed during the shutdown. I was too nervous to even go outside and run at the beginning.

By the month of June, I was completely out of shape! So, let's just say getting back into shape for a marathon was no fun and all WORK!! When I started training, my legs were tight and I was in so much pain because I hadn't been doing any working out. But I knew the task that was ahead of me and I was willing to put in the work and do whatever it took to get back in shape. I ended up running almost every day and completed 100 miles during the month. Then, I turned around in July and doubled my miles. I ran every single day, even after a long run, no matter how sore I was. By the end of the month, I completed 200 miles! In the past, a typical month of training is only 70 miles. But with only two months of training after being totally out of shape, I ran 26.2 miles the second week in August.

Some people called me crazy for running a marathon without any spectators or receiving a medal. But those people don't understand what I gained mentally and physically. I learned what I was capable of doing, a lesson that held more value than receiving recognition. Knowing that I improved myself holds more value than a medal any day!

I have a burning desire inside of me that looks for challenges and disciplined practices in order to succeed. I even ate only plant-based food during that summer, just so that I could discipline myself to only fuel my body with what it needed and not with what I wanted. I would like to say I was able to train for only two months and complete a marathon because I chose plant-based food but I have no proof. I just know that I felt really good and accomplished something I've never done before. I challenged myself to complete 300 miles in two months then run a marathon the very next month. And because of my discipline and hunger to Win, I achieved what I set out to do! Some people might not count that marathon, but when I tell people how many marathons I've run, I will still count it because I know the work I put in to complete it.

If we don't learn how to commit to ourselves when it comes to our personal goals, how will we ever learn how to commit to ourselves when it comes to our Dreams? I pledged to myself that I would do two marathons during 2020, and that's just what I did. In October, I ran another 26.2 miles though for that one I received a medal from the Marine Corps who sponsored the race. I did a virtual marathon and just had to show proof of the 26.2 miles that I ran. Some may call me insane for running two marathons in a single year, but *I'm just HUNGRY!!!* I truly have a burning desire inside of me that looks forward to doing whatever is necessary to become better than who I was yesterday.

How can you get to the next level without self-development? You can't! How can you prepare yourself for all the obstacles that come along while fulfilling your dream if you don't prepare yourself mentally? You can't! It is so important for you to seek new ways to improve yourself and prepare for the future because that will give you the confidence and fortitude that's needed to continue to go after your dreams even when obstacles arise. *As you continue to grow, so will your vision.* Self-development allows you to grow in the areas where you are weak and strengthen the areas where you are already capable.

I make sure that my personal goals mirror my professional goals by accomplishing what may seem impossible or too hard to achieve. When I set a personal goal that once seemed too hard yet I achieve it; I then take what I learned and apply it to my professional goals that may seem impossible or too hard to accomplish. I don't choose the easy way for myself because I know that going after my dreams will also be challenging.

In 2019, as I was training for the Marine Corps Marathon, it was time for me to run 20 miles for my long run. That level of conditioning fell on September 8th which was my late mother's birthday. In honor of my mom and also a way to challenge myself, I ran the entire 20 miles with no music. As I ran for four hours straight, I used that time to think about my mother and all the memories we've shared. I just used every second, every minute, and every hour thinking about how much she sacrificed for her family and how she created a life for us that she felt we deserved. She honestly gave me memories of a lifetime. I cried, I laughed and I just talked to her while I ran. In those four hours I just wanted to honor her and share that time thanking her for being such an amazing mother.

Music is a big part of motivation for people working out and I must be honest, I didn't know I could run that long without music to distract me. But at the end of the run, I learned once again, you never know what you can do until you try! Because I continue to challenge myself, I am now at the point in my life where I've shown myself on numerous occasions that I can do whatever I put my mind to. I honestly go through life feeling like there's NOTHING I CAN'T DO! I purposely wake up every day, asking myself what I can do that day that I used to believe I couldn't do.

I learned how to build self-confidence by setting personal challenges for myself. Every challenge that I set is a reminder that going after all of my dreams and aspirations won't be easy either. We all have to accept that in the world where we live, we are always going to have challenges. We are always going to have hardships and disappointments. So why not prepare yourself, mentally, physically, and emotionally?

Life is going to happen and the quicker you are able to accept that fact, the more you will be willing to prepare yourself for what's to come. You have to be RESILIENT! Resiliency allows you to always be in control over you and your circumstances. Being resilient allows you to stay focused by remaining mentally and emotionally stable. Being resilient causes you to have that burning desire on the inside of you to WIN! You only focus on what you can change and you're constantly willing to work on yourself, even in the midst of a storm. You have to change your thinking in order to be resilient. You have to be able to see past your circumstances. You have to know that you are capable of overcoming any obstacle you face. When you make the decision that giving up or accepting mediocrity isn't an option, you gain the confidence to know you are more than capable. You tell yourself that you deserve all that God has for you despite the circumstances you face.

> *I can be changed by what happens to me.
> But I refuse to be reduced by it.*
>
> —Maya Angelou

In the first chapter, I asked, "Who Are You?" Again, it's so important that we truly understand who we are and what we want out of life so that when difficult circumstances surface, the core of who you are isn't affected. You are able to understand and identify when life is happening and you use those moments to go after your dreams with a burning desire deep inside of you. When life happens, that's when you have to show up for yourself even more. When obstacles arise, that's when that hunger on the inside of you makes you feel like you're starving. Hunger is something that cannot be given, it is a burning desire that can only be acquired from within. When you are hungry, you are more committed, dedicated, disciplined, and resilient towards your goals.

When life tries to get the best of me, I really become tunnel visioned. I only can focus on my goals and the dreams that are in front of me. In 2020, my marathons got canceled but after seven years of training, I decided to run 200 miles in a month for the first time. That was my way of saying, to the pandemic "Oh, no problem that they are canceled. Let me go even harder!" Having that attitude helped me to navigate the hardships that the world was going through. Instead of accepting that we were in a pandemic, I told myself daily that I was going through a **WINdemic**! It was important for me to keep a positive mindset and continue to stay focused on my goals. I knew I couldn't be consumed with what was going on around me and I made up my mind that no matter what, I was going to continue to *WIN!* You have to be so hungry for your goals and dreams that you are willing to fight for your own potential. You are willing to put in the EXTRA that goes in front of ORDINARY. If you don't fight for your potential, then who will? You have to stay hungry for the next best thing you want to happen in your life.

I truly make winning so personal because I owe it to myself to get all that I believe I deserve out of life. It's personal for me because at one point of my life I accepted losing as my normalcy and I didn't fight hard enough to win. I robbed myself from numerous victories because of the restrictions I placed on myself. And now, I refuse to do the bare minimum when it comes to my happiness and my success. Being good is no longer acceptable anymore! It is a MUST that I become GREAT in everything I choose to do. I don't want to be a good mother, I have to be a GREAT mother. I don't want to be a good author, I have to be a GREAT author. I don't want to be a good runner, I have to be a GREAT runner. Good isn't good enough for me anymore.

The more I challenge myself, the higher the standard I hold for myself. The only person who is getting in the way of you and the life you desire to live is YOU! If you don't like your current circumstance, then YOU need to change it! Begin to set higher standards for yourself because people will treat you the way you treat yourself. The expectations that you have for someone else should never be higher than the expectations that you set for yourself. Three small steps that you can take that will allow you to always hold yourself to a higher standard are:

1. Hold yourself accountable
2. Set small goals that will allow you to work on your weaknesses
3. Be your biggest fan and cheerleader

We can't leave our happiness behind and expect another person to make our dreams come true because it will never happen. If life has really been a roller coaster for you, trust me, I know how you feel. I know it can be frustrating and difficult to push forward, but you owe it to yourself to fight! To fight for what's yours and beat the odds that are set against you.

Can I be completely honest with you? Running is not easy and I won't lie to you and say that it is. I don't love to run but I do love the person that I've become because I run. The challenges that come with running have shown me how to persevere. No matter how you feel, no matter how difficult the task at hand may be, you have to continue to stay the course. You have to continue to push ahead and only focus on what you are working towards. Perseverance will help you focus on the rainbow instead of the storm you may be going through. You learn how to keep control even when life gets rocky. Don't allow anyone or anything hold you back from what you want to achieve.

There are so many different elements in life that will try to discourage you! The Devil is always trying to catch you in high waves of Fear that will try to take you under. Sometimes the Devil succeeds and you end up feeling like you are drowning but as long as you have breath in your body, you live to fight another day! You just have to keep kicking!

We often assume just because we fall short, we are supposed to stop pursuing our dreams. It's a constant battle to keep pushing each day we wake up! There will always be distractions in our lives, but we can't allow for those distractions to take precedence over our dreams.

Being hungry is about moving forward, no matter how many times you get knocked down. Just imagine your full potential positioned at the top of a mountain and as you walk, jog, run, or even sprint up the mountain, there are boulders thrown at you. You sway from left to right to avoid being smashed but eventually one hits you and the boulder pushes you to the very bottom. You might think to yourself, "Dang, that hurt and now I have to start all over." Most people don't want to start over because of the time that they already invested. Others might be afraid of being hit again and experiencing the pain they felt the first time. Fear can block your vision and make you want to give up.

Your thought process will play a major role in you wanting to try again. Only you have control over your thoughts and how you choose to perceive unfortunate circumstances is key. Instead of thinking about your recent loss, you must consider how you can turn that loss into a lesson learned. How can you come back better and stronger than before? That mindset will help you avoid getting hit by the same boulder again. Even if we get knocked down by a different one, we have learned from our previous experience.

When we get pummeled by life, we only want to focus on the fact we just got knocked down. This is why we play the victim card and waste time feeling sorry for ourselves. Yet, no one wants to focus on the fact that when you get knocked down in life you also have the opportunity to grow wiser and stronger. You become more powerful and better equipped so that over time, you are able to dodge the boulders that are thrown at you. Eventually you will be able to see the boulders coming before they are even thrown. You become aware and then you prepare yourself for what's ahead. Every time you get knocked down, there is a lesson gained that will move you closer to your dreams.

If we just change our thinking to always see the good in every situation, we can take advantage of the moments we think are losses. I'm so addicted to winning that I still find a way to turn my losses into wins. Winning in life is a mental challenge and as NBA great Kobe Bryant said, "You have to have a Mamba Mentality," to reach above and beyond expectations, no matter the circumstances. He also said to make sure you do the simple things *right!* Sometimes that simple thing may just be showing up for life and making your dreams happen one step at a time. We sell ourselves short when we try to cut corners. What seems easy isn't always the best route for you to take. In order to be great in anything, you have to start somewhere. We should master one goal before we try moving on to the next level. Doing the simple things right is about establishing a strong foundation for yourself. Learn to commit to a goal and see that goal through. Stay Focused! Stay the Course! And Push forward no matter what!

Follow-Through and Execution is Key!

As I take a look back at my life and compare it to the next person, I realize that my journey took longer. But what I learned in the process caused me to grow as an individual and took me to the next level. We want everything to happen immediately and winning just doesn't work that way. In cosmetology school, I always thought I would be a platform artist who traveled across the world and did hair shows. But my journey didn't take me in that direction, it took me another route. Instead of a platform artist, I became a dual-licensed professional barber and cosmetologist, a best-selling author, and a seven-time marathoner. Working, training and giving all that you have to offer is what it takes for you to get to the next level. That burning desire on the inside of you is your indicator to go as hard as you can until you can't go any harder.

Don't just Dream anymore. Believe and make those dreams happen. You must go after your dreams by telling yourself that accomplishing them won't be an easy task. The Devil will take every opportunity to distract you. Have you ever wondered about the times in your life when everything was going smoothly for you and then out of the blue, your ex-girl/boyfriend contacted you? Of course, you look at your phone and say, laughing to yourself, "Not today, Devil, Not today!" Understand, the Devil will go the extra mile to put roadblocks in front of you and distract you from your dreams. He places people and situations in your life that will throw you off your focus and take you off your task at hand. Once you've experienced setbacks in life, you will be able to identify when the Devil is trying to use people and things to distract you.

Mistakes are only detrimental to you when you choose to continue to make the same ones over and over again. Mistakes allow you to grow as an individual and cause you to push through other obstacles ahead. We must take advantage of every opportunity that allows you to gain insight and enjoy the growth that takes place in the process. Leverage your setbacks in life and use them to fuel you!

The hunger inside you will cause you to have a sense of urgency when it comes to your goals and your dreams. In Les Brown's latest book, *You've Got to Be Hungry,* he writes about having a RIGHT NOW URGENCY! Don't wait until it feels right or you know how you will make your dreams possible, just start working on them Right Now!

Before reading his book, I always told myself, "Jenise, you have to have a sense of urgency when it comes to your goals and your dreams. You can't wait for people to understand your vision or wait for others to give you the okay to proceed." I had to understand that the longer I procrastinated, the longer it was going to take me to accomplish my goals. I couldn't focus on my current circumstances or how I was going to make my dreams a reality; I could only focus on just starting the process.

> *You don't have to be Great to get started but you have to get started to be Great.*
>
> — Les Brown

The quicker we understand and accept that life will happen, the better off and the better prepared we will be when obstacles arise. It doesn't matter how many times you've been knocked down. As long as you are willing to fight, you will eventually be able to take what is yours. When all the odds are against you, just make sure you get more than even.

Reflect & Refocus Key Points:

- Being Hungry isn't given, it is only acquired from within
- The process is where you grow and evolve
- A positive mindset will allow you to always have control over your thoughts
- Do the *"Simple Things"* right!
- Have a Right Now sense of urgency when it comes to your goals
- Follow-Through and Execution is Key!
- Stay HUNGRY for the next best thing

No one should want a better life for you then you want for yourself. Being Hungry will always ignite that fire on the inside of you to go after what you believe you deserve. Hunger is about digging deep down within and pulling the greatness out of you! It's time to become Hungry for your future and what God has for you!

When you fight for your full potential, that's when you make the impossible possible!

<u>Non-Negotiable</u>

Sacrifices will have to be made but your Dreams should never be something that is sacrificed.

—Jenise McNair

Your dreams should never be up for Negotiation. Not now, not *EVER!* Once you've figured out your purpose in life, you will realize that your dreams are non-negotiable. Your dreams are aligned with your purpose in life, so you can't have one without the other. There's a reason why your dreams are so important to you. Your dreams are placed in your vision and in your heart because your purpose in life put them there.

Our purpose is what fulfills us in life. Purpose causes us to wake every day knowing exactly what we are supposed to do. Understanding that aim motivates you to account for every second, every minute, and every hour. Your purpose is all the power you will ever need in life. No matter what you've been through or the setbacks you've encountered, your purpose will always be your purpose.

Your purpose doesn't disappear because of your shortcomings. Instead, your purpose is magnified even more when you fall short. Sometimes, we allow the obstacles of life to make us feel like we have to sacrifice our dreams, but because your purpose remains in place, drawbacks should not stop you. We all have to get to a place in life where we truly accept that we will fall short at times. We are going to make mistakes and poor decisions or go in certain directions in life that we shouldn't travel. But even through all of our mishaps in life, our purpose is what causes us to fight to get back on track.

At one point, I struggled to provide for my three children as a single mother and felt like I dropped the ball. I never wanted to be in a financial position where I wasn't able to give my children what they needed. I thought my goals and dreams weren't going to ever happen. I wondered, "How can I pursue my dreams and still do what I need to do for my children? Is going after my dreams, knowing I have three children, selfish of me?" My children had their own hobbies and sports activities that they were interested in, so as a single mom, I didn't see how I could focus on both their dreams and mine. It's a natural feeling for parents to accept that once they have children their dreams aren't a priority. I believed, at the time, that my dreams should no longer matter and that pursuing them made me a selfish mother.

But as time went by, I finally realized going after my dreams and bettering myself, was also going to benefit my children on so many levels. Through my own journey of healing and trying to become a better version of myself, I recognized the best way to teach my kids or to show them the right way was to lead by example. How could I tell them to always follow their dreams and don't ever give up if I didn't stand true to my own words? I had to start living a life that I believed in. I wanted my children to know their dreams are possible by watching me go after mine.

Throughout the years, I chose to put my children's dreams first and mine second. I realized that in order to make my dreams a reality as a single mom of three, I had to make certain sacrifices. But I discovered that sacrificing my dreams couldn't be an option. Instead, I had to sacrifice my sleep, sacrifice pleasurable hobbies like shopping, and most definitely, sacrifice dating. How could I honestly make time trying to get to know someone when my time was already limited? I either could use my free time to date or use my free time to go after all of my dreams and aspirations but I couldn't do both. Great sacrifices had to be made but I knew that my dreams couldn't be one of them.

Prioritizing is so important if you want to maximize your time. My children's dreams and my dreams were at the top of my priority list. I also made sure that I kept God as my focus as well! Anything else wasn't worth sacrificing for and still isn't. I tell myself often, "You must focus on what you want *most* instead of what you want at the moment." Your priorities in life truly show what's important to you. Your priorities take precedence over everything else.

Chasing my own dreams and making them a priority ended up benefiting my children and me because I was able to tap into my greatness. I stepped out of my comfort zone and used my gifts and talents as a female barber to create a better financial situation to provide for my children and myself. Following my dreams gave my children hope and aspirations to go after what they love to do as well.

Your Dream is a priority and it is not Negotiable! Do not sacrifice your dreams. Do not negotiate your dreams or give up on them. Life happens. So yes, you will have to adapt when unfortunate circumstances arise but you should never give up on your dreams. Learning how to adapt will allow you to readjust and stay in control of the task at hand, even while experiencing roadblocks. Adapting causes you to be flexible with situations that take place unexpectedly and allows you to keep moving forward no matter what.

Adaptability is about the powerful difference between adapting to cope and adapting to Win.

— Max McKeown

We all have something special to give to the world and some people realize what that special gift is a lot sooner than others. This recognition goes back to the importance of knowing who you are! There is only one of you in the entire universe. People may try to impersonate you but no one will ever be able to duplicate you. We can't take our individualism for granted. The qualities that someone possesses determines his/her individuality as a person. Our unique personalities are what separate each of us from the next person.

One person's personality can be someone's else's light in their time of darkness. Being in another's presence at the right time and at the right moment can truly save that person's life. You never know what someone else may be going through. Your purpose in life could be sharing your character with others. Unfortunately, some people have a very negative household so meeting someone with a loving, warm, and positive spirit can really be like a breath of fresh air. Being exposed to different perspectives is great, especially when you only know what you are surrounded by.

Have you ever had a bad day when everything went so wrong but then you ended up being with someone who made you laugh deeply? In that moment, you forgot all about your problems, worries, and circumstances. In that moment, you were surrounded by positive vibes, laughter, and joy. You can truly create happiness in the midst of a storm. And you can't allow unfortunate circumstances to control your emotions and cause you to react in a negative way. No matter what obstacles come your way, you should never let drawbacks cause you to question your purpose because your purpose is part of who you are.

Everyone's purpose in life isn't destined to be a famous celebrity. Not everyone has a purpose that will be shared with people around the world. Some people's purpose is fulfilled at their job, on a bus ride home from work, in the grocery store, or even as the coach of a sport. Our purposes may not be the same but no one's purpose is more important than the next person's.

I believe that our dreams are connected and aligned with our purpose in life. If you have a dream of having your own school, owning your own beauty salon or barber shop, growing a business empire, or developing a community center for youth, you must do whatever is necessary to make your dream a reality. My pastor once said, "Your purpose is always connected to someone else's need." His statement resonated with me and it left an imprint in my heart. There's someone out there who needs you to fight for your dreams and fulfill your purpose because their life depends on it.

Once my pastor spoke those words, I knew it was essential for me to fulfill my purpose and finish my best-selling book, *Potential of a Man vs. Truth*. Its publication has truly been a blessing because it allowed me to be transparent and help other women across the world embrace and walk in their own personal truths. I knew that my purpose was connected to other people so it was important for me to share my story with women who had similar circumstances to mine. It was a dream of mine to become a best-selling author, but my true purpose is to impact other lives and that is what mattered most to me.

After my book was published, so many women reached out to me just to say, "Thank you," and to tell me that my story gave them hope. Receiving those messages is what I value most and they give me confirmation that I am doing what I'm supposed to be doing. *I'm walking towards my Purpose!*

Our dreams are aligned with our purpose in life. Your dreams can't be sacrificed or negotiated. Your purpose should come naturally to you; it should feel organic. Your purpose should never be something you have to try and figure out how to do. Your purpose is actually something that you do quite often. When you think about the great legends like Michael Jackson, Whitney Houston, Kobe Bryant, and Chadwick Boseman, consider all the impact that they made. That influence was only possible because their dreams were non-negotiable. They fulfilled their purpose by sharing their special talents and gifts with the world. Think about how music touches the soul or how sports figures inspire youth to work hard in a sport that they love. Seeing someone follow and actually live out their dreams gives you confirmation that your dreams are also possible. They fought for their dreams and because of it, millions and millions of people's lives were impacted.

Our dreams are not supposed to be a fantasy that we wish could happen. Our dreams are supposed to be a part of our life's plan and we must do what's necessary to follow through. A dream without a plan is just a fantasy. When we set our goals and make a plan, we should always follow through. When you don't follow through, you give up on yourself and you also let down those around you; the people who are paying attention to you from afar and rooting for you. People are always paying attention, even when you don't notice. Our decisions in life don't just affect us but they also affect the people closest to us.

It was imperative for me to stay focused on my goals and my dreams during the pandemic because the shutdown gave me valuable time that I couldn't afford to waste. The Covid-19 pandemic was life-changing in every aspect of our lives and although I couldn't change what happened around me, I still had control over the effort I made towards reaching my dreams and goals. As a single mom with three kids to care for, my job loss during the Covid shutdown was unexpected. I had to make sure that I used my money wisely, knowing my financial circumstances were uncertain. Even as I drew unemployment, my dreams were still non-negotiable, though trust me when I say, I was not mad about being on unemployment! I took any extra money I had and continued to invest in myself and my future. I knew that writing another book would cost money but I couldn't let my job loss get in the way of my dreams. Job or no job, I was determined to continue with my scheduled program.

As I mentioned before, life is going to happen and you must learn how to adapt. We can't anticipate what will happen in life that we have no control over but you don't have to participate in the emotional stress either. When I woke up every day during the pandemic, I didn't think about not having a job. All I focused on were the goals that I set and what I needed to do to accomplish them. My routine didn't change. My vision didn't change. And most importantly, my hustle didn't change. Having that routine benefitted me because it allowed me to transfer my focus, my dedication, and my energy into working on my own business and connecting to my purpose. If I had allowed my job loss to make me feel anxious and stressed out, I wouldn't have been able to see the opportunities that helped me grow personally as well as in my business.

When God closes one door, you better believe that He will open another. Losing my job showed me that I needed to always be in control of who pays me. It gave me the choice to really dive into entrepreneurship on every level. I also had time to study so I could go get my realtor's license. Having different streams of income is important and I was determined to come out of this pandemic even stronger, better, and wiser than before. Losing my job wasn't a negative element. In my eyes, I needed this time to work on my dreams and my Legacy!

Oftentimes we allow our circumstances to get the best of us and we become so consumed with the circumstances we aren't able to change. Focusing on an unfortunate situation hinders your ability to change and adapt because it will cause you to shut down mentally, emotionally, and physically. And when that happens, you allow yourself to remain stuck. In order to move forward, you will have to address your hardships but that doesn't mean you have to wallow in them. How you choose to respond when life happens will dictate your outcome. You have to stay the course and focus on your game plan. This focus allows you to be resilient and ready to accept change because you have a full understanding that obstacles will arise and challenges will come but that should never stop you from pushing ahead and getting what you believe is yours.

You can't negotiate your dreams even when it comes to being on the other end of that negotiation. You can't allow your fears to get in the way of you making your dreams a reality just because your current circumstance isn't ideal. I refused to tell myself that because I lost my job, I shouldn't focus on my dreams. I couldn't tell myself that my dreams needed to be put on hold. With all that was happening in the world, it was important that I went even harder to fight for my future. I was fighting to live to up to my fullest potential. I needed to continue doing all that I could to make sure I'm never again in a financial position where someone else determines when I work or especially, when I get paid.

This pandemic was an opportunity for growth. It was an opportunity for me to work on taking my life to the next level. Because I have been on my own personal journey, working on personal growth and becoming the greatest version of myself, I've become disciplined in every aspect of my life, including dealing with money. Prior to losing my job, I saved up enough money so that I'd never worried about being able to pay my bills, despite my job loss. As a matter of fact, when I received my unemployment payments, I was able to put it straight into my savings account. So, even at a time when I had every reason to be worried, sad, and scared, instead I was focused, hungry, and positive. I didn't allow my emotions to make me feel like I needed to renegotiate my dreams.

> "For I know the plans I have for you," declares the LORD, "plans to prosper you and not to harm you, plans to give you hope and a future."
> — Jeremiah 29:11

Don't make permanent decisions based off temporary circumstances. Allow your hardships to fuel and motivate you to go after what you desire to have. No matter what you are going through, I need you to understand that your dreams should never be negotiated just because you are having some challenges. Life can be complicated, frustrating, difficult, and uncertain but one thing is for sure: **YOUR DREAMS MATTER!** Your dreams will never matter more to someone else than they matter to you! You have to carry the attitude that your dreams are always going to be on the top of your priority list.

The pandemic and the lives that were lost showed me just how important it is to go after my dreams and live the life that I desire because tomorrow isn't promised. People take that statement for granted but every day, I wake up telling myself to live life with no regrets! The year 2020, wasn't a year for living in fear or questioning our purpose; 2020 was a year that should remind us that our Dreams can't wait! They can't be put on hold! We need a right-now sense of urgency when it comes to our dreams and fulfilling our purpose.

Are you in a position where you question whether or not you should still pursue your dreams based on an unfortunate circumstance that took place in your life? Do you feel as if your dreams are impossible to reach? When disappointments take place in your life, they tend to discourage you and make you feel defeated. You wonder how you can pursue your dreams when you are faced with so many obstacles. In the midst of adversity, that's when you have to work the hardest! That's when you will need to invest in yourself the most.

When you try to overcome challenges, that isn't the time when you should give up and give in; that is the time when you allow your hardship to fuel you and push you forward! You must allow those challenges in life to ignite that burning desire inside of you to Win! **At all costs you must Win!**

Nothing is more powerful than a winning mindset! How can a person with a winning mindset be defeated? They can't. Because no matter what obstacles may come their way, they know that all storms must come to an end. And while the storm is taking place, they never stopped working towards their dreams. Fight through the storm!

Life can't stop just because you experience hard times. *Challenges bring forth growth!* Life is like a big obstacle course; each phase of your life becomes more challenging as you continue to move forward. Life doesn't get easier, you just get better over time. You become more aware of your surroundings and you learn how to navigate through the obstacles. When you get knocked down you make a mental note of what knocked you down and how it impacted you. You consider what you could've done differently and then you try again!

We make life so much harder for ourselves when we allow our emotions to control us and get the best of us. Our emotions play a major part in our decision-making. When we get caught up in how we feel that's when we start negotiating our goals and dreams. Allowing yourself to lose control and letting fear take over is what hinders your focus to Win.

No matter what you are faced with, your dreams are non-negotiable! Your dreams are a part of who you are so when you choose to give up on them, you are choosing to give up on yourself. We all make great sacrifices in our lifetime but our dreams should never be sacrificed. Choosing yourself doesn't make you selfish; instead it means you are smart. You are investing in yourself, whether with time, money, or focus. If that commitment involves you growing and evolving into the greatest version of yourself; there's no amount of money, time, or focus given that wouldn't be worth the cost. You are going after your dreams and fulfilling your purpose.

Reflect & Refocus Key Points:

- No matter your age or circumstances, your dreams are **NON-NEGOTIABLE!**
- Your dreams are aligned with your Purpose
- Your purpose doesn't disappear because of your shortcomings

- Adaptability is the difference between adapting to cope or adapting to win
- Your purpose is Necessary!
- Your purpose is connected to someone else's need
- Fight for your Dreams because some else's life depends on it
- **YOUR DREAMS MATTER, SO MAKE THEM A PRIORITY!**

Despite all the upheaval that took place in 2020, I encourage you to live a life with no regrets, to focus on your inner happiness, and to give all that you have to make a meaningful impact in this world. Winning in life should always be at the top of your priority list, no matter how many storms you face! Work on you! Bet on you! And don't ever stop moving forward because Your Dreams Matter!

When you fight for your full potential, that's when you make the impossible possible!

Winning Circle

*Measure success by how many people
are successful next to you.*

—Jay Z.

Growing up, I was a social butterfly and I loved going outside straight after school. The only reason why I even went home was to drop my book bag by the front door. Going outside never got old; even after being outside for six hours I was so mad when those street lights came on and we had to go in the house. Kids today have no idea what that outside life is all about; all they care about is video games and staring at a screen. My parents didn't know, but after school I used to make my friends these special homemade buffalo wings, using a recipe that my brother taught me. They were so good! Even now, my friends still ask me to make those wings when we get together.

As I look back at my childhood, I truly cherish those memories with my friends. Believe it or not, in this present day, I still have 90% of my childhood friends, who I now consider my family. They are stuck with me forever. I'm 34 years old and I have more than a dozen childhood friends that I've known for over 20 years. We literally grew up together from little kids to teenagers to adults. Of course, my kids call all of them Auntie and Uncle. They aren't my biological siblings but they have all been in my children's lives since birth. Love is a choice, loyalty is a choice, and being supportive is a choice. That bond is what our relationship is based on and all that we've given to each other to withstand 20 years of friendship. Like any other relationship in your life, sacrifices have to be made and you will have to be selfless in order to preserve life-long friendships. Unfortunately, over the years, some friendships grow apart and they don't withstand the changes that occur in life yet it's okay.

I believe people are put in your life for reasons and seasons. Who you were as a child and what you are interested in changes over the years. I've seen situations where friends grow up and simply drift in different directions. The choices that we make can affect the ones around us. So, if the direction that your friends are going isn't beneficial to you and doesn't serve the goals you have, then unfortunately, that friendship no longer adds value to your life and you may need to let it go.

Loyalty will cause you to choose between what's best for you and what's best for your friends. Loyalty may make you feel guilty for doing what's best for you! That attachment is called misplaced loyalty! Misplaced loyalty is detrimental because it justifies not doing what's best for you and putting the loyalty to someone else higher up on your priority list. Misplaced loyalty can cause you to lose sight of your own values, morals, and ambitions. It's so important to have people in your life who will always have your best interest at heart.

Many friendships are broken because people decide to make positive or negative changes in their lives. Your friends may want to go to the club every weekend and spend unnecessary money but maybe you'd rather go to the gym to stay in shape or save your money because you are trying to buy a house. Then of course, here comes the guilt trip from your friends: "You really changed lately. You are not the same anymore!" Your friends aren't lying; you are changing and you aren't the same person anymore but that's only because you're growing and you want something better for yourself. As we age, our thinking should change as we start to look at life with a different set of lenses. What we thought was cool when we were younger, was actually kind of stupid; we realize this fact as we get older. Not everyone grasps this lesson at the same time. Our own life experiences and journey cause us to want to make some changes at different phases of our lives. Yet, not everyone grows or experiences self-development at the same rate.

Like any other relationship, when two people don't grow together, they end up growing apart. When that happens, effort will need to be made on both ends so they can figure out how to get back on the same page. Many friendships are lost because there is no compromise or only one person is willing to put in the work that's needed for the relationship to flourish. My friends compromised with me when we were in our twenties, knowing there wasn't much that I could do because of my circumstances. I was the first in my group to have a child but instead of going to the club, they were fine coming over and bringing food, drinks, and playing cards. They never wanted to leave me out but instead they found a way to include me.

Now that my children are older, a lot of my friends are married or are in committed relationships. I don't get mad because their free time is limited due to the fact that they have spouses. I respect where they are in their lives and we make time for each other when we can. What I cherish the most about our relationships, is that no matter what is going on in our lives, if we ever pick up the phone and need anything, we are always there for each other, no matter what! I am blessed to have a group of friends with whom I was able to learn and grow along my own personal journey.

My childhood friends are a part of my *Winning Circle*. Your winning circle is a group of people who play a major role in you Winning! As much as we may think we can achieve our dreams on our own, the fact of the matter is, we can't. It is so important to have other people to support your winning journey because we have to accept that we don't know it all. Each person has strengths and weaknesses but with a winning circle you can capitalize off each other's strengths to become better. We have to put our pride to the side and understand that we can't win alone.

Pride comes before the fall.

— Proverbs 16:18

I know you've heard the saying, "You are who you hang around." The company you keep will determine the level of your success.

What I love about my friends is that we are all so different but we are also one and the same. We are all very goal-driven and ambitious. We all have our own dreams and aspirations, but we feed off each other's energies. One of my childhood friends always keeps me abreast of his goals and game plans. And I'll never forget when he shared with me everything that he wanted to accomplish. He wanted to sell his car to save money, pay his debt off, buy a house for his mother, and own his own restaurant. Because I had known him for such a long time, there was no doubt in my mind that he would achieve these goals and I was excited for him! This man did everything he said he was going to do and watching him achieve his goals was mind-blowing. But in order to accomplish this dream, he had to create a blueprint first.

I vividly remember sitting across from him at my kitchen table at 4 am as he expressed all the goals he wanted to accomplish in a certain time frame. Then, I watched for two years as he caught Übers and lifts everywhere. He had always had a brand-new car since he was 16 years old, so going without one was a *Big Deal.* He bought his mom a place, paid off all his debt, bought himself a new car, and he now owns his own restaurant. He did everything he said he was going to do and I'm telling you, out of our simple conversation, he was able to manifest every one of his dreams.

The average person only sees the external fruit of someone else's labor but I witnessed the struggle he endured to make his dreams a reality. I witnessed the sacrifices he made because he was more focused on what he wanted in the future than what he wanted at the moment. His grind and his hustle motivated me even more to make sure I worked just as hard for myself. He held me accountable without even realizing it, just by doing what he needed to do for himself first. He is the type of person I need in my Winning Circle because he pushes me to be better just by working to improve himself.

What's amazing is that he isn't the only one of my friends who operates with that winning mentality! I have friends who are entrepreneurs, a basketball agent, a lawyer, a police sergeant, the CEO of a non-profit organization, those who hold high government positions, a restaurant owner, a talented and gifted underground DMV artist, a nurse practitioner, real-estate agents, and directors. And not to toot my own horn, but I am a Best-Selling Author and seven-time Marathoner! My entire circle is Amazing! We all want to work hard and achieve big in life by feeding off each other's ambition.

The company you keep is important so there might come a day when you have to distance yourself from those who do not add any value to your life, regardless of how long you've known them. You can't surround yourself with negativity or people who drain your energy every time you are around them. Maybe they are always angry or always complaining. If you continue to surround yourself around that type of people, you will soon take on their negative mindset and lose sight of your goals and dreams. You need people in your life who will help you get to where you are trying to go, not those who hold you back! Positivity brings forth Prosperity! Someone else's energy can inspire you or drain you. You have to surround yourself with people who are going to make you better!

Your winning circle won't just include your friends and your family but should also include a mentor or people who have achieved what you would like to accomplish. Include those that you network with or others in your field. Read books by authors who are already successful at what you want to achieve.

When I was in the process of writing my first book, a good friend of mine told me about her book coach because she was writing a book as well. She mentioned that having a book coach would help the process of finishing and publishing my book much smoother than trying to do it on my own. My friend and I always talk about our goals when we get together, but this particular conversation pointed me to the path that led me to become a best-selling author. Although, having a book coach was costly, it was an investment that I felt was necessary and I knew my dream was worth it. My book coach was amazing and I appreciate my good friend who connected me to her. She doesn't know it, but I consider that friend as a mentor to me. She's older, wiser, and clearly has way more connections than me! She didn't have to give her secret for easy publication but she wanted me to win and made sure I was connected to the right person so my dream to complete my book became a reality. My book coach is a ten-time, best-selling author so she was just the right person for me to connect with.

As much as I thought I could make my dreams happen by myself, I realized that I needed to study the Great in order to be Greater. My desire to be a nationally known Motivational Speaker can't happen without studying the greatest motivational speakers. I understood that I needed to invest in myself if I wanted to go places I've never been before. I needed a Mentor, someone who lived through the journey and trusted the process.

For years, I was aware of the top motivational speakers. Les Brown was always someone I listened to when I needed to hear some encouragement. During the pandemic, I enrolled in his Power Voice Training. There I was, spending more money, knowing I didn't have a job! But I believe it was Divine providence for me to come across this training that he presented for the first time. The pandemic gave him free time to train and pour into other aspiring motivational speakers, like me. Being on a personal zoom call with a legend like Les Brown was mind-blowing! I was able to hear more of his life stories that he has never shared before and they showed me that he was very humble despite his fame. He wanted it to be known that with the right attitude and hunger inside, there's nothing we can't achieve.

The amount of money he told us that he made (prior to the pandemic) to travel out of the country and speak for just one hour was unbelievable. What he earns to speak within the States for an hour could equal someone's yearly salary, *times two*. Those figures didn't discourage me but instead, they ignited that burning desire on the inside of me to Win and follow my dream to become a motivational speaker. I loved it when he stated, "Some of you will be even Greater than me!" because he made my dreams stretch even further.

Les Brown made me realize that our purpose isn't something that we choose to do; instead our purpose is what we were born to do. Being in that training showed me that there were so many other like-minded people who were just as passionate as I am about wanting to inspire others.

Les Brown wasn't the only motivational speaker I trained with. I also took advantage of every opportunity to engage with other great motivational speakers in the industry, like Eric Thomas and Lisa Nichols. They offered free online webinars and training courses that I made sure to take advantage of. Each speaker was able to give me tips and tools that will help me on my journey to become a Motivational Speaker.

I want to learn all I can from the best motivational speakers because they all offer me something different. These differences help promote a winning circle because everyone's uniqueness is what allows us to see with a different perspective in mind. It helps us to always be open to new ideas and strategies to Win! They all have their own special gifts to share with the world. I don't want to miss out by only focusing on one motivational speaker. They all have their own unique style and I am able to gain so much from each of them.

I listen to many of them in order to learn and be inspired. Eric Thomas is very passionate and speaks with so much conviction. He makes me want to go outside and tackle somebody because he is so passionate about winning! He doesn't allow you to make excuses for yourself and he holds you accountable for the actions you aren't taking to make your dreams a reality. He just gets you so pumped up and reminds you that you don't have time to waste.

Lisa Nichols has a very similar story to mine. She was a single mom on welfare and her son's name is Jelani just like my son! But she fought for her potential and went from needing welfare to become a Millionaire! She reminds me that being a mom is my motivation to go as hard as I can for myself and, most of all, for my children. She never gave up! *She is a BOSS!*

Les Brown speaks from a place of humility and hunger. His passion inspires you to beat all the odds stacked against you. His humor and wisdom soothe you and he has a way of making you want to reflect on yourself. Les Brown leaves you motivated and hungry for more.

After a day of listening to these three speakers you will be **FIRED UP!!!** You will feel like you can take on the world and will be mad that you wasted so much time. Each of these speakers activated the ambition inside of me and inspired me to do more. I consider these three motivational speakers my mentors. They all possess great knowledge that can help take me to the next level of my career. Having a mentor who's walked the steps you are trying to take, allows you to avoid the mistakes they once made.

Trying to achieve your dreams by yourself can be the difference between accomplishing your dreams in ten years versus one to two years. Having a mentor helps you avoid mistakes and reach your dreams much faster. There are successful people who are willing to give out their blueprint to win. You need to cherish that blueprint, study it, and apply its wisdom to your life.

One thing is for certain, you may not like some celebrities or highly paid successful people but you have to respect their hustle because they did whatever was necessary to *Win!* And they did not accomplish those results on their own. Instead, they were in the presence of people who helped them achieve their dreams.

In his Power Voice Training, Les Brown spoke about associating with **OQP** (Only Quality People). These are the people who can take you places that you cannot go by yourself. He mentioned that it could be hard to find nourishing relationships in your current environment. If that is the case, then you may need to get into a better environment!

Your loyalty can be detrimental if you aren't strong enough to separate yourselves from a group of friends just because you've known them for a long period of time. Knowing someone for a long period of time means absolutely nothing, especially if they aren't adding any value to your life. That connection just sounds like valuable time wasted, due to misplaced loyalty.

We have to be comfortable with making difficult decisions that will help us grow as individuals as well as elevate our level of success! Unfortunately, we don't have time to wait for others to catch up to the level you are on, in terms of trying to better yourself! Waiting for others may hold you back from advancing further. You don't owe anyone that level of commitment that will only cost you your dreams in the end.

Now I want you to take a moment and think about the company that you keep.

Ask yourself:
- Does my circle of friends add value to my life? Or do they take away from my life?
- Does my circle motivate me, hold me accountable, and support my dreams? Or does my circle put me in compromising situations that they know aren't best for me because they are only thinking of themselves?
- Does my circle push me past my limitations and challenge me to grow by mirroring their ambitious efforts? Or does my circle make excuses for themselves which allows me to justify my own reasons to settle for less as well?

I can't emphasize enough how important it is for you to know who you are and to make sure you surround yourself with like-minded individuals. IRON SHARPENS IRON! People who don't think up to your level can't help you go to the next level. Your winning circle may not be composed of the friends you had growing up and that's okay. Sometimes loyalty causes us to hold onto relationships because of time but those relationships aren't nourishing. You can't allow for your loyalty to others get in the way of your own personal growth. Your loyalty to someone else should not cost you your dreams or opportunities to advance to the next level. Trust me, I bleed loyalty, but I also know that my friends' happiness should never come before mine.

God has blessed me with a winning circle that always has my best interest at heart. Those friends are able to tell me what I *need* to hear instead of what I *want* to hear. We don't always agree but our respect, love, and loyalty towards each other always bring us to an understanding of our differing opinions. Recognizing different opinions and being able to accept hard truths from your friends will help you continue to win because we don't always know everything.

There will be times in your life when you might need someone to tell you that you are wrong or that you aren't giving your all. If your friends can't be honest with you or tell you hard truths, then you don't really value true friendships. The truth may be hard to hear from them but the truth is always necessary to better yourself! True Friends won't let you walk around in False Realities.

True friends celebrate your victories as if it was their own. The day I became a Best Selling Author with my first book, *Potential of a Man vs. Truth*, one of my sister-best friends said to me, "I am so happy and excited right now, you would think I wrote the book!" I deeply felt those words because they reminded me how genuine my winning circle is. **WHEN ONE WINS, WE ALL WIN!**

You have to surround yourself with people who are passionate about obtaining a Winning Life. There will be people who come in your life for a short amount of time yet they will significantly add more value than someone you've known for decades. We have to recognize the people who help us move forward as well as those who hold us back. Life will cause you to make difficult choices, but within those difficult choices, there will always be opportunities for growth.

Humility allows you to accept that you can't make it to the top on your own. There are people who are put in your life that will lead and guide you on your journey of success and will help you to avoid mistakes along the way. It's natural for us to feel or want to do everything in our own power but being successful is truly a joint effort within your Winning Circle.

Reflect & Refocus Key Points:
- Make sure people add value to your life and don't take away from you
- Learn to be okay with letting go of others whose time no longer serves purpose in your life
- Surround yourself around **OQP** (Only Quality People)
- Find a Mentor for guidance and knowledge

- Be open to different perspectives and new ideas
- Learn to accept hard truths from friends/family
- Make sure you have like-minded people in your Winning Circle

Take heed of others who've walked your path and know what it takes to be Great! Study them, mimic them, and pay attention to the steps they took to get to where you want to be. Remember, your winning circle is a group of people who are on the same path as you or are where you would like to be. If you surround yourself with successful individuals, you will soon become a successful individual yourself!

When you fight for your full potential, that's when you make the impossible possible!

Learning & Mastery

Don't be afraid of experiences that stretch you, challenge you, and give you opportunities for growth.

—Jenise McNair

Whenever I found myself in a low place, I always felt like that was God's way of trying to get my attention. We have all had moments in our lives when a certain circumstance causes us to question, "Why Me?" It's natural for us to allow our emotions to only focus on the negative aspect of our circumstances. But we must change our thought process and understand that every low and high in life is just an opportunity for learning and mastery. Changing our thought process takes time but it all starts with how we choose to think!

Everyone experiences the peaks and valleys of life. When you are at the top of a mountain, you have mastered that phase of your life but when you are in the dip, that is just an opportunity for you to grow and learn new lessons. When we go through hardship or are at the lowest point of our lives, that is when God is saying it is time for you to grow in this particular area of your life. As you begin to grow and learn, that's when you start to climb that mountain. Then once you reach the top of that mountain, there will be an even bigger mountain that you will have to climb next. These mountains represent the long uphill climb that the changes in your life will offer you. We will always have opportunities given to us to grow but we will also face obstacles and storms along the way. Being at the bottom of a mountain can seem very frustrating and overwhelming as you try to figure out how you will make it to the top. But how you learn through your life's challenges will help you climb and thrive.

I have experienced many low periods in my life and for some of them, I didn't take advantage of the opportunity to grow. I was only able to focus on how I felt instead of appreciating the experience. When I lost my mom, I didn't use that opportunity for growth; I could only focus on the pain I felt. This focus on my own pain, in turn, caused me to remain at that lowest point in my life a lot longer than I should have. I was STUCK! I couldn't move and honestly, I don't think I wanted to.

Have you ever experienced a period of your life where you were at a low point and instead of trying to come out of it, you just wanted to wallow in your misery? Staying in that low place somehow makes you feel better but it doesn't help you change your circumstances. Wherever you are in life and whatever experiences that you are encountering at the moment, this is your opportunity for growth. If you feel down and stressed out about your job, this is the opportunity for you to figure out what you really want to do. Being at a job that causes stress and makes you feel depressed isn't a job you should continue doing.

As a mom of three, I get it when people claim they need their dead-end job that pays the bills. I truly understand when you feel like your back is up against the wall and you don't have a choice but to remain in a job that doesn't bring you happiness. It doesn't matter what your experience is, you always have a CHOICE!

Several years ago, I taught at various cosmetology schools over a ten-year period of time. I enjoyed waking up every day, knowing I was a part of those students' journeys in becoming Cosmetologists. I went to school every day, no matter what was going on in my home. I made sure I motivated my students to keep pushing forward, no matter how challenging or difficult the classes were. Some of my students had children they raised alone and had a hard time finding daycare. Some of them dealt with personal traumas at home and others were homeless, living out of their cars. Many students looked forward to school because that was the only piece of happiness they had in their lives.

While teaching, I had my own drama going on at home and tried to balance the toxicity in my life. But I knew every day, I had to walk in that school and give those students the very best of me. Yet I couldn't give the best of me, only what I was able to give at the time. At home, it felt like I faced constant thunderstorms but whenever I went to work, I always acted like the sun was shining on me. There in the valley and at the lowest point of my life, I was still able to help others rise up out of their own valley and climb to the top.

When hard times hit, we can't just subsist through it; we actually have to learn through those moments instead. When we make a choice to just get by during difficult circumstances, we actually allow ourselves to be complacent in where we are. We wake up every day and go through the motions, feeling sorry for ourselves. Complacency is not healthy or productive because it stops you from growth. And when growth isn't present, you stop living.

During the most difficult time of my life, I just went through the motions but life didn't get any easier for me; it actually got worse! While in that valley, I experienced the loss of my mother, entered a toxic and abusive relationship, suffered financial hardship, discovered new insecurities from weight gain, and put my health at risk. Most of those experiences could have been avoided had I made the choice to *learn* through my circumstances instead of choosing to just *live* through them. I allowed myself to go from one valley to the next.

I honestly feel like the death of my mother is what caused me to be stuck in several valleys. Losing my mother made me feel like winning in life was no longer an option for me. I experienced one of the biggest losses in my life and I didn't think I could come back from it! I got accustomed to thinking that I would never experience reaching the peak of my mountain again. I got used to being at the bottom of life and I made myself as comfortable as I could be.

If we never take the time to learn from our mistakes, we will only continue to make those same mistakes. I felt inspired by my students and the progress they made, even while they faced difficult circumstances at home. Despite what I dealt with outside of work, I knew I needed to do something different in my own life. I'll never forget the day I taught class and told my students not to limit themselves. "Do all that you can, the best way that you can," I said, "so you can always be in a position to make money."

As I spoke, my own words started to resonate with me. I also needed to stop limiting myself! I was already a cosmetologist and I'd always wanted to be a licensed barber as well, but my daughter's father never wanted me to. However, that same week, I broke off my engagement with him. We got into an argument because he kept coming into the house at inappropriate hours. I just finally realized I needed better and I deserved to be with someone who respected me. So, as I told my students not to limit themselves, I realized that I needed to take my own advice.

After my decision to move forward in my life, I was forced to make a lot of difficult choices in a very short period of time. In order to go back to barbering school, I had to resign from teaching. My life was in shambles; I was a single mom of three, going through financial difficulty and trying to heal from my painful truths. Yet it was important for me to take a chance on myself and go to the next level of my career. For years, I encouraged and motivated my students to go after their dreams, despite their circumstances. And now, I realized I had to go after mine. Leaving my students was hard but they supported my decision to further my education and career.

Although it was not an easy choice, going back to get my barbering license was one of the best decisions I could have ever made. That step was my start to no longer being complacent at the bottom of the valley and finally making the effort to push forward up my mountain. That choice was the point when I started to fight for my own potential. In life, hard times can cause us to feel stuck; they can make us feel like the life we desire is impossible. Going back to barbering school changed the game for me.

I became a dual-licensed professional which allowed me to separate myself from the next person. Not only was I able to service Mommy and Daughter but I was now able to service Father and Son. I understood that as a woman entering a male-dominated industry, I couldn't just be good. I had to strive to be Great! But I was afraid I wouldn't be good enough. I feared I wouldn't be considered a respectable barber because I was a woman. Yet, I couldn't allow fear to stop me from excelling in my career. And that one decision opened so many doors for me and put me in a financial position to take myself off public assistance.

I received a job opportunity to work at a hair restoration company where they serviced both men and women. There were 17 other licensed stylists at the company and one other female barber who was retiring from her 21 years of service. I walked into this opportunity as the only dual-licensed professional. My skilled qualifications made me very valuable and highly requested within a short amount of time working there. Men were amazed and appreciative of how I cut their hair. I started making more money than I'd ever earned before, a welcome change from my financial struggles. Bringing home $1300 a month in just tips was a big upgrade! I take pride being a female barber and I always give my clients a five-star experience. Because I chose to fight for my full potential, I unleashed the greatness inside of me and became a phenomenal female barber!

You see, when the chips are down, you can't allow for your emotions to control you. I could have very well allowed my break-up, my financial struggles, and my fear of being a complete failure to control me. I could have continued to wallow in misery but I knew it was time for me to confront my fear and face the world, with all odds against me. You can't allow yourself to be complacent, accepting mediocrity or less than what you deserve. Every day is a constant fight to press forward and overcome the obstacles that come your way.

I learned valuable lessons while experiencing those particular lows of life:

1. It's important to be around people who believe in you and want to see you win.
2. Never give advice to others that you don't take for yourself.
3. There will always be someone else who has hardships that are much worse than what you are experiencing, so stop feeling sorry for yourself.
4. When you fight for your own potential, you make the impossible possible.
5. You are only stuck when you choose to stop moving forward.

No matter what you are experiencing, no matter how you feel, no matter who said you couldn't, **YOU MUST CONTINUE TO PUSH FORWARD.**

So often, we look at our circumstances as setbacks but in reality, our circumstances are opportunities given to us for growth, opportunities that will stretch us and cause us to gain wisdom. Learning is an integral part of life and most people remain stuck because after a certain age, they aren't open to learning anymore. The world is always changing and evolving and you can't allow your ego or pride to stunt your growth as an individual. Always be open to learn something new. Be open to trying and discovering new ways to become better.

If you experience a challenge, whether it's mental, physical, or emotional, that only means there's room for growth in that area of your life. I tell my friends and family all the time that I don't enjoy running. But I enjoy what I gain from running. Running allows me to stay in great shape, I am more cognizant of my health, and I learn to overcome obstacles that challenge me physically and mentally. And most of all, running lets me experience accomplishments I felt were once too hard or impossible.

That perspective is how we should look at life; every experience that we encounter is an opportunity to show us exactly what we are made of. When you try to achieve a goal, that undertaking shapes and molds you. That is the phase that challenges you to bring out your inner fight. You might get discouraged; you might become tired or frustrated. You might even start to question your ability to achieve your goal. But in that same process, when you decide to move forward, no matter how you feel, that's when you discover your strength, your courage, and your determination. You realize that you are more than capable of doing whatever you put your mind to. The process never gets easy but you definitely become stronger.

We have to get to a place in our lives where we can accept that obstacles will come. But how you choose to respond to those obstacles will determine your outcome. People don't become great overnight; they become great by continually practicing and by learning from their mistakes. Yes, mistakes can hold you back but only if you allow them to. Mistakes are only discoveries that make you aware of what not to do the next time. Mistakes bring awareness! If you change your thinking, you will honestly change your life.

Trying again, in any area of your life where you've made multiple mistakes, will help you to apply what you've learned so you get better. Every time you fall short in life, the wisdom you gain from your failures allows you to master that particular area of your life. After you've fallen so many times, you are able to overcome in the area you've failed. That's how mastery takes place. People become masterminds in their particular specialty because they know what it takes to Win in that area. They know the amount of effort, dedication, consistency, and determination that is needed to Win. They've experienced multiple mistakes so they know what it feels like to fail in that area. They were only able to become a mastermind because they chose to keep fighting and they continued to push forward, using their discoveries as their weapons.

Every day that you try is another day that you get better. Think about a time when you told yourself you were going to start a new journey, a journey that made you test yourself and change. Perhaps a challenge that forced you to make a significant effort towards breaking your bad habits. Maybe you decided to work out, eat better, drink more water, or stop drinking or smoking. The first day is always the worst day! Think about the day you started to work out for the first time. Of course, you felt like you wanted to fall out and your heart beat out of your chest. Think about when you told yourself to avoid fast food because it was time for you to start making healthier decisions. You chose a salad for dinner but the whole time, all you wanted was a cheeseburger and fries. Think about when you grabbed a bottle of water yet as you drank it, all you wanted was some juice instead.

Most of the time when we try to break bad habits, we fail before we succeed! The first day you do great, and the second is even better. Then on the next day you slip up and get off track! At this point, most people go back to their old ways and fall back into the same routine. But for those who truly want something better, although they messed up, they choose to get back on track and try again!

There is no success without experiencing failure first! When I first started running, it felt impossible to run three miles without stopping. And trying to convince myself that I could run 26.2 miles seemed out of the question. But the process of trying gave me hope, courage, and strength to keep pushing forward until my goal was achieved.

Today, I have mastered the ability to set goals and achieve them. I honestly just apply the same work ethic as the one I use to run my marathons. Every time I challenge myself, I learn something new about me. I accept there will be difficulties but I set small milestones and do whatever is necessary to complete those milestones no matter how I feel. Going through the process to achieve a goal always reveals qualities about myself that I didn't know I had.

Many people ask how I am able to achieve the goals that I set out to accomplish with all that I have going on in my life. I don't lie to myself about the process or the level of difficulty I may face trying to accomplish my goals. I truly just take each step, one day at a time, and set milestones within my goals. Most importantly you have to have a daily routine that causes you to be disciplined and consistent. The problem with most people is that they have unrealistic expectations about the goals they set out to reach. They live in a false reality and aren't honest about where they are in life while trying to accomplish their goals. Everyone wants their dreams to take place overnight. They are anxious and not patient when it comes to wanting results.

I've mastered goal setting because I truly embraced the process that it takes to achieve my dreams. I remain in control of my emotions and I don't mismanage the available time that I have to work on my goals. I coach my clients about the importance of execution when it comes to achieving their goals. It is essential that they are always in control and set realistic deadlines that align with their current lifestyle. When you allow yourself to get overwhelmed, that's when you might feel defeated and give up.

There is a dream that has been placed in your heart for years. Life keeps knocking you down and you feel like your dream is so far from becoming true. Your losses in life are taking a toll on you and you feel stuck. But I want you to know you can't give up! Mary Mary's song, "I Just Can't Give Up Now," is amazing! The lyrics truly touch your soul in those moments when you feel defeated.

> *I just can't give up now*
>
> *I've come too far from where I started from.*

Nobody told me the road would be easy

And I don't believe He brought me this far to leave me.

Reflect & Refocus Key Points:

- Mistakes are necessary for growth
- There's no success without experiencing failure first
- When you've reached the top of a mountain, that represents your growth in that particular area of your life.
- Valleys are learning opportunities
- Change your mindset to look at mistakes with a positive set of lenses
- Despite difficulties, giving up should never be an option
- Turn your Mistakes into your Mastery!

Can you think of one celebrity who achieved success yet has a story of how their achievement was easy for them? Nothing in life worth having will come easily. But reaching that mountain top will definitely be worth the climb! Learning is a big part of life's experiences and growth opportunities. Your losses in life are only lessons learned. The sooner you understand that, the sooner you will become unstoppable. So turn your **Mistakes** into your **Mastery!**

When you fight for your full potential, you make the impossible possible.

UNLEASH

*Greater is He that is in me than he
that is in the world.*

—1 John 4:4

I truly believe that fighting for your full potential will be the toughest fight of your life but it is also the most rewarding. It is the only fight where you will experience both Wins and Losses but you gain the courage and the strength to fight another day. In the chapter Be Hungry, I compared the fight for your fullest potential with climbing to the top of the mountain while boulders are thrown at you. Those boulders represent challenges, hardships, circumstances, and obstacles that life will hurl your way. Trying to obtain your full potential in life, will never be an easy walk in the park. The quicker we accept that truth, the better we can prepare ourselves for the fight that's ahead of us.

In the movie, Creed II, Adonis Creed was the son of the legendary fighter Apollo Creed. Thirty years earlier, Apollo fought the dominating Russian boxer Ivan Drago and died in the ring after a terrible hit. Apollo's friend and trainer Rocky Balboa went to Russia to avenge his death and defeated Drago! Adonis Creed grew up to follow in his father's footsteps and became a great boxer. After winning the Heavyweight Champion of the World title, Adonis was challenged by Viktor Drago, the son of Ivan Drago.

Viktor Drago was big, strong, and a powerhouse in the ring. He knocked out every opponent he fought within four rounds. His father trained him to fight for blood and to take every opponent down with his powerhouse punches. Most of all he was trained to take out Apollo Creed. He was, in fact, HUNGRY! This challenge was his way of defending his father's name after his defeat by Rocky. Yet for Adonis Creed, the fight was also personal because he felt the need to avenge his father's death!

On the day of the fight between Adonis Creed and Viktor Drago, everyone was nervous and scared about the outcome. As soon as the fight started, Drago baited Adonis and started to attack him with his big, powerhouse punches. Adonis' trainer wanted to call the fight off but Adonis refused. By Round Three, Adonis' ribs were broken and one eye was swollen shut. He clearly didn't have the strength to continue the fight while Viktor looked like he hadn't been touched! Adonis allowed his emotions to overpower his good sense and he kept fighting. During the Round, Drago attacked Adonis with his power punches and as Adonis fell to one knee, Viktor hit him with a mean uppercut which knocked Adonis out. Drago, however, was disqualified for hitting Adonis while he was down.

When I first watched that movie, I perceived it from the point of a person who knows exactly what losing feels like. But I understood why Adonis lost; he let his emotions control his actions! All Adonis could think about was Viktor being the son of the man who killed his father. During his training, he never once considered Viktor's weight, height, strength, or skills. Adonis' entire regimen was based on his emotions and feelings. Adonis didn't lose the fight because Viktor was disqualified but anyone who watched that match knew Adonis lost when comparing the level of skill. He didn't lose because he was smaller; he lost that fight because he was led by his emotions and didn't prepare himself better.

How many times have you allowed emotions to get the best of you and you only made a decision based off how you were feeling at the moment? It is imperative that we prepare ourselves for the obstacles and challenges that we are going to face. We are often driven by our emotions and we make permanent decisions based off temporary circumstances. We have to make sure we aren't consumed by emotion when life doesn't go as planned. It's okay to acknowledge how you feel for a moment but you cannot stay stuck in your emotions. It is so important to prepare ourselves mentally for the trials and tribulations that will come our way.

By failing to prepare, you are preparing to fail.
— Benjamin Franklin

We don't lose in life because we aren't capable of winning. We lose in life because either we don't know how to win or we don't do what it takes to win. Period! Being emotional in the times of distress causes us to lose our focus. And when that attention is lost, trying to prepare for what's ahead isn't a priority. When you lose your focus, you begin to work against yourself. You can't move forward if you only concentrate on how you feel instead of considering where you're trying to go.

Most people who experience a big loss in life give into their emotions and feel defeated. Although you may have suffered loss in a particular area of your life, there was so much that you gained unknowingly. When we focus on our losses in life, we don't take advantage of the lessons that are placed right in front of us. We miss out on the opportunity to grow and become better, all because we are so consumed with how we feel. You can't allow your emotions to interfere with your game plan. Yes, it's natural to feel defeated after a loss but remember, when you have a winner's mentality, **YOU ALWAYS WIN!**

When I lost my job during the pandemic, I had every right to want to panic, especially with three kids to take care of. But instead, I instantly felt like God was giving me time to work on my business and my Dreams. I was in control over my emotions the entire time because I have come to a place in my life where I know obstacles are never-ending. There will always be a challenge thrown your way. Keeping my emotions in check and choosing how to respond, allows me to always be in control over my life, no matter what I come up against.

I looked at my job loss from every positive angle and I didn't have to force it; I have conditioned my mind to always be as positive as possible, no matter what circumstance arises. When you work on the inside of who you are first, what happens on the outside can never interfere with what takes place internally! Working on myself and learning who I am has helped me discover how to calmly channel through challenges. I understand that I may not always be in control of my circumstances but I am always in control of how I choose to respond to those circumstances.

Nothing should ever get in the way of you unleashing the greatness that's inside of you! Many people desire to be great but they just don't know how to unleash their greatness! Throughout my journey of healing, learning, growing, owning, and taking accountability over my own life, I've figured out a success model that has allowed me to WIN, no matter what I face. You should work the hardest when you find yourself in the midst of adversity. You are going to be tested day after day and week after week but there is still a way to navigate through life without allowing your emotions to get the best of you. In order to always be in control over your emotions, to focus on your goals and achieve them, you will have to dig deep down into the **D.E.P.T.H.S.** of who you are.

- **Discipline** yourself to do what you've never done before
- **Execute** and follow through with a game plan to achieve your goals
- **Persevere** through the obstacles and challenges
- **Trust** and embrace the process
- Have **Humility** that will allow you to learn from others
- **Self-Development** is the foundation of your success

When you think about the life you desire and all of your dreams that you want to make your reality, ask yourself, "What am I willing to sacrifice to reach them?" Unleashing your Greatness within will take great sacrifice and dedication. Will it be easy? No, but we shouldn't want it to be easy anyway! *You should never choose the easier route if the harder route will make you better!*

I wish I could tell you that my road to success has been easy but it hasn't. When I think about all of the battles that I had to fight to become the person I am today, it was my greatness within that allowed me to persevere and overcome. There were days when I woke up and I didn't know how I was going to make it through the day. Hitting rock bottom when you only have to care for yourself is tough but hitting rock bottom, knowing you are responsible for three other lives, was demoralizing. I had to heal the scars from my childhood trauma of sexual abuse, the death of my mother, an abusive, toxic relationship, and financial struggles.

At times, those challenges felt impossible to conquer. But I owed it to myself to show up and push through. Every day, I was willing to fight so that I could change the narrative of my story. My infinite strength and fortitude allowed me to continue to try, even when life placed stumbling blocks in my way. My future and my children's futures were dependent upon the effort I was willing to make to become the greatest version of myself, despite the odds that were stacked against me. Fighting for my full potential and unleashing the greatness on the inside of me gave me the courage to keep pushing forward and fearlessly going after my dreams, despite my circumstances.

I am often asked, how do I balance all the responsibilities that I have, as well as find the time and energy to go after all of my dreams and aspirations? But I always reply, "When you Choose You, that's when you will be willing to do whatever is necessary to make your Dreams a **Priority!**"

In *Creed II,* when Adonis Creed decided to go back up against Viktor Drago for a rematch, he had to think differently. More importantly, he had to do something he'd never done before in order to secure a different outcome the second time around. He agreed to train with Rocky, who took him to a secluded desert. This time, he wasn't focused on his emotions; instead he was centered on his strategy to Win. Rocky challenged Adonis with a series of grueling drills in the heat of the day which forced Adonis to grow and learn how to persevere through the pain.

Despite the challenges that were thrown at him during training, Adonis started to believe he was BIGGER than his circumstances! He mentally started to tap into his Greatness from within. His mental strength became more dominant than his physical strength. He started to train like the

Champion he believed he was! By time he finished training in the desert, not only was he physically prepared, but most of all he was mentally prepared to take on one of the biggest fights of his life.

We must understand that we ALL are bigger than our circumstances. The mental battle in any situation is so important because it allows you to get out of your own way. Learning how to break mental barriers causes you to do what you never thought you could. Mental toughness will always outweigh your physical capabilities. You must develop mental toughness in order to endure the ongoing challenges that will consistently be thrown your way.

On the day of the fight, Adonis was emotionally disconnected which allowed him to focus on winning the challenge ahead. As the first round started, Viktor used the same strategy as the first fight. Yet, he wasn't fighting the same person as previously; his opponent was a man who was quick, strategic, and Dangerously Hungry! Adonis ended up dominating the fight and showed he was the true champion. As Drago's father realized his son couldn't take anymore, he threw in the towel to end the fight. Adonis Creed defended his belt and remained the HEAVYWEIGHT CHAMPION OF THE WORLD! The difference between this fight and the first one against Drago was his mindset and preparation. Adonis realized that he was worth fighting for his own potential and no longer had to live in his father's shadow.

Your mindset and preparation will allow you to overcome obstacles a lot quicker than expected. Some people say they always prepare themselves for the worst but that perspective causes you to operate with a negative view towards life. Instead, I say, always prepare for the best but just be prepared that the worst may still make its appearance. Unleashing your greatness within will allow you to digest hardships more easily because you accept that life will have its moments of uncertain battles. So, continue to fight within and believe that you are more than capable of giving your very best so you can become your very best self.

In life, we have to figure out our 'Why.' We can't want our Dreams to become a reality to please someone else. You have to go after what you want for yourself! *You don't owe anyone anything but you do owe yourself everything!* Fighting for your potential allows you to reveal qualities about yourself you never knew you had. That goal requires you to give all that have to give, in every aspect of your life. It pushes you past the limitations that others place or that you put on yourself. When we believe in ourselves and fight for our potential, that's when we make the impossible possible. You owe it to yourself to show up and show out for yourself; to go above and beyond and to be willing to make sacrifices for yourself. The amount of effort that you choose to put into yourself is the **STANDARD!** Nothing is more important than working on you!

We have to allow our potential to produce greatness! You owe it to yourself to become everything you've ever dreamed of being, no matter how many roadblocks in life try to stop you. Let your setbacks in life fuel you to beat the odds stacked against you.

In 2020, I had to run both of my marathons virtually due to the pandemic. While training for the Marine Corps marathon, I ended up straining my quads while trying to race my fourteen-year-old son. At the time, I didn't realize sprinting causes you to use very different muscles than a typical run. I was told that in order to heal, I needed to stay off my legs and not do anything but rest. But I knew I still had one more marathon to complete. I couldn't just sit back and do nothing but I did have to cut back on my training some. While running, I could tell that my quads were strained because my typical runs that are usually easy were uncomfortable. But I continued to push anyway. My training throughout the years enabled me to develop a level of mental toughness that makes me capable of pushing through any physical challenges. I've mentally conditioned myself to follow through with any task I set out to complete, no matter how I may feel.

The original race was set for October 25th but the virtual race gave participants a window to run the 26.2 miles any day until November 10th. I told myself that I would run my 26.2 miles on October 25th, no matter what the weather conditions were. When I awoke the morning of the race, it was cold and rainy. I said to myself, "I just can't get away from cold and rainy marathons." The year before, I ran the marathon through what felt like a tsunami!

My dad called and asked me if I was still considering running since it was such a cold and rainy day. I responded, "Yes, I am still going to run because if it wasn't a pandemic and I woke up to run my marathon, I would still have to run in the rain and cold." He reminded me that I could just choose a day to run when the weather was better but I was already determined to run on October 25th, no matter the weather conditions. My family begged me to reconsider and couldn't believe I decided to run on such a terrible day, especially when I could choose a better day. But I am a woman of my word and I was determined to follow through with what I said I was going to do.

So out into the cold and rain I went. By mile 13, I was chilled and soaking wet. My quads started to hurt but I expected this to happen since I never fully allowed them to heal. Realizing I had thirteen more miles to go under these conditions, I had to tap into my mental strength, despite how I felt in the moment. I had to allow my mental capabilities to take control. As much as I wanted to walk, I recognized that the slower pace would lengthen the time for me to finish. Yes, I was in pain but I chose to keep pushing forward and not once did I walk until I got to mile 20. I walked then only because I had to stop to get something to drink! Up until that point, I hadn't had anything to fuel my body. The only thing that fueled me was my mindset to keep going, no matter how I felt. When you mentally lock into your goal, you don't let anything get in the way of what you said you were going to do!

After I chugged down some Gatorade, I continued running, although I couldn't feel my legs. My adrenaline kicked in as I told myself, "You only have six more miles and you will complete your seventh marathon!" Believe it or not, those last six miles were some of the fastest miles throughout my run. When I reached 24 miles, my dad called to check my status. "I only have two miles left, Daddy!" I told him. He cheered me on over the phone, "You're almost there!"

During those last two miles of the race, I didn't think about the fact that I couldn't feel my fingers, my legs, or my toes. All I focused on was the fact that I ran this marathon, even though I wasn't at my physical best and the weather wasn't either. When my running app registered my 26.2 miles, I instantly stopped and said to myself, "Jenise, there isn't anything that you can't do. Don't ever allow yourself or anyone else to tell you otherwise!"

My dad walked up to me and he placed a medal around my neck, saying, "You are one determined woman and I'm so proud of you!" Then he said, "Next year, I am going to run a Full Marathon myself!"

I replied, "Really Daddy? I'm going to do it with you!" Two years earlier, I inspired him and my sister to run their first half marathon. Knowing that I still inspire my dad at 66-years old to push himself even more, truly touches my heart.

Unleashing the Greatness within you starts with believing there's actually greatness on the inside of you to be unleashed. We all have something special to give to the world but I'm a firm believer that you must learn how to walk in your personal truths before that greatness can be unleashed. Our own personal traumas, insecurities, unhealed wounds, and negative surroundings hold us back. Fear, doubt, and trials also play a part in confining what is meant to be shared with the world. But God put brilliance on the inside of you that only you have the power to release. You have to align your actions with the goals you want to achieve by fully understanding what's needed for you to follow through and execute your process.

Two years ago, I was in training about a month before my marathon. On this particular Sunday, it was imperative that I run 17 miles so I could stay on my training schedule. It was pouring raining outside but my only other option was to go to the gym and run on the treadmill. Now, I truly despise the treadmill because there's no scenery and running on a machine for a long period of time is so redundant. The furthest I ever ran on the treadmill was around five miles. The thought of running on the treadmill for 17 miles made me delirious! But my choice was either to run outside in the pouring rain or to try something I never thought I could do.

Well, I chose to challenge myself and run on the treadmill. The first five miles went fine but after that, it was a mental battle to keep going. I had to mentally lock in on the task at hand and choose to ignore my feelings which tried to consume me. Several men asked me how many miles I was running because they knew I had been on the treadmill for a long time and they couldn't believe my response. One worker told me, I inspired him to work on his health and fitness. If I could run 17 miles on a treadmill for over 3 hours, then he knew he could commit to running for 30 minutes a day.

When I started my run, I had no idea people were watching me. I was amazed at how fulfilling a challenge to myself impacted others at the same time. I realized I would've never known how long I could run on the treadmill had the weather been better. That was a day that I unleashed a part of greatness in me that I wasn't aware that I had. Fighting for your full potential really shows you just how great you are, especially when you're willing to challenge yourself. And that greatness makes an impact on those around you, whether or not you think they are watching.

You can't unleash your greatness without commitment. It's going to take struggle, determination, and dedication but you have what it takes to get it done. Learning how to commit to yourself plays a major role in unleashing what's on the inside of you. There are two types of commitment: your internal commitment and your external commitment. Your internal commitment has everything to do with what you say you want to do. Your internal commitment is controlled by your mind. I made an internal commitment to myself to run a Marathon. An external commitment has everything to do with your actions! This decision requires physically making an effort to work towards what you internally committed to, then doing whatever is necessary to see it through. My external commitment to running a marathon was actually making the effort to train, eat healthy, and be dedicated so I could follow through and complete the race. Your internal and external commitments go hand-in-hand. You can't commit to one without committing to the other! For instance, you might internally commit to eat healthier food. But your external commitment requires making the effort to stop eating fast food and consciously being mindful of how you prep for the meals that you cook and eat.

When you tell yourself you're going to do something, you have to follow through. Say what you mean and mean what you say. We rob ourselves from truly living out our greatness within when we aren't willing to commit to ourselves! *If you never learn how to fully commit to yourself, you'll never learn how to fully commit to anything.* Staying the course through the ups and downs of life will give you the sincere reassurance that your Dreams are still possible.

Reflect & Refocus Key Points:

- Don't allow your emotions to dictate your actions!
- By failing to prepare, you are preparing to fail
- When you have a winner's mentality, you always **WIN!**
- You have to dig deep down in the **DEPTHS** of who you are: Discipline, Execute, Persevere, Trust, Humility, and Self-Development
- You owe it to yourself to always show up and show out for yourself
- If you never learn how to fully commit to yourself, you'll never fully commit to anything
- There are two types of commitment; **Internal** (mental) and **External** (physical); they both go hand-in-hand.
- You have to give your very best in order to become your very best self.

- Only you have the power to **UNLEASH** the Greatness that's inside of you

Unleashing the greatness within you is really determined by your willingness to take action. You must truly believe that you have what it takes to be great at whatever you set out to do! Give yourself a chance to really see who and what you are made of. You hold the power to unleash the greatness that God placed inside of you and it's time that you get out of your own way! You have a choice to be strong or weak because life is going to consistently try and test you! But you can't allow the elements of life to hold you back.

Everyone has greatness on the inside of them but each individual's greatness is uniquely special! Embrace that you are remarkable and that there's no other person like you. Unleashing your greatness within will show you that you are more than capable of making your dreams a reality and will spread hope to other people along the way!

When you fight for your full potential, that's when you make the impossible possible!

WINdemic

*You just can't imagine a better future,
you have to FIGHT for it!*
—President Barack Obama

WINdemic - a breakout of victories and triumphs that becomes contagious amongst others around you!

For every loss you experienced in life, there's truly a journey ahead that leads to nothing but WINS! But you must be willing to fight for it.

I believe everyone has what it takes to become Winners and I'd rather be at the top, sharing victories with my friends and family, than at the top celebrating alone. I am a lover of people so it was really hard for me to get to a place in my life where I could accept that not everyone will like me. It's a harsh reality but it's the truth. Likewise, not everyone has a positive outlook either, but it's okay because we already know we don't live in a perfect world. There will always be battles we will have to fight. But fighting for your future should be your Number One Priority.

While going through the pandemic of 2020, I told myself to make sure that no matter what was happening around me, I had to continue to fight for my future. Millions of jobs were lost, and so many people passed away due to Covid-19. Then, during the summer we even had to fight against the Police Brutality that took place, yet everyone came together to push the BLM (**BLACK LIVES MATTER**) movement and create change. The cry for justice was very emotional to deal with but I knew the problems of America wouldn't change overnight and couldn't consume all of my time, emotions, and energy. I always felt that doing my part to help change the world required focusing on me and changing myself for the better first.

When we focus on our own change and development which unleashes the greatness on the inside, we open up opportunities to experience nothing but Wins. While going through the pandemic and confronting my job loss, I thought to myself, "God is intentional; He doesn't move me forward to push me back." I worked three jobs, averaged about four hours of sleep each night, and wasn't able to really spend the time I wanted with my children. But then, I was blessed with an opportunity that allowed me to work 100% remotely from home and paid six figures, definitely an upgrade! Being able to pick my children up from school every day, be at home to start dinner early, and actually eat with my children was a blessing. I finally knew what it felt like to have a work/life balance.

Losing my job during the pandemic was definitely shocking but I knew God doesn't give us good to take it away. If He takes it away it's because he has something better for us! Going through the transition doesn't always feel that way. Sometimes God takes away what's good but does not replace it with something better right away. Sometimes God allows us to grow into someone better instead. You know that old saying, "Give a man a fish, you feed him for a day. But teach a man to fish and you feed him for a lifetime." God gave me an opportunity to really see why managing my finances is so important.

When I lost my mom years ago, I honestly stopped caring about everything. I was nonchalant about paying my credit cards which in turn, hurt my credit score. In this time of financial struggle when I wasn't able to feed my children, I didn't even have a reliable credit card to help me. I had to fight to get my credit back together.

I realized that I needed to make some major changes in my life. My sister Talia really helped me get my finances in order and made me understand the importance of buying what I needed and not what I wanted. She is very good with managing her money so I respected her advice. I asked for her help because I knew God wasn't going to bless me with more money if I couldn't manage what I had.

The discipline I had with my fitness goals started trickling over to my finances. I only bought what I needed and anytime I wanted something outside of the necessities, I had to save for it. So, when the pandemic hit and I lost my job, the good habits that I developed about managing my money came in handy. Being responsible and disciplined with my finances helped me when it mattered most. While dealing with the pandemic, I still challenged myself to save the most money I've ever saved in my life, almost 20k! I worked hard to be disciplined with my finances and I became **Debt Free!** I didn't owe anybody anything and it felt so good! My credit was restored to an excellent rating and I was approved for two credit cards with a balance high enough for me to buy two brand new cars if I wanted to. I didn't apply for those credit cards to spend; they are only in case of emergency. The pandemic taught me even more to always have a back-up plan. My children and I didn't miss a beat during the pandemic because of the solid financial habits I developed.

God has given me the opportunity to be in the best financial situation I can possibly be in and now I have the time available to work on my own business. He allowed me to be ready to put myself in the position to always be in control over my finances. It was time for me to go to the next level of being an Entrepreneur. Losing my job wasn't a setback, it was an upgrade. It was an opportunity for me to level up and fight even harder for my future.

Working on every aspect of my life was in my best interest! I never thought saving money was possible but when I challenged myself and fought for my own potential, I revealed qualities about myself that I didn't know I had. Working on yourself gives you an opportunity to grow in so many areas of your life so that you can Win!

Set a goal so big that you can't achieve it until you grow into the person who can.
— Will Smith

Back in 2010, after I lost my mom, my dad told me he was about to lose our family home because he couldn't afford it on his own. Experiencing the loss of my mom really hit my family hard. My dad asked my sister and brother how they felt about letting the house go into foreclosure. They said it was fine and to let the house go. But when my dad called me and asked me the same question, I lost it on the phone, saying, "Daddy! You can't just give up like this! How can you let go of the only thing that we have left of Mommy? I know the mortgage is too high for you alone but you can't let this house go without a fight!"

Many years earlier, my mom was determined to move her family from the city out to the suburbs. My dad told her that they couldn't afford the house but that didn't stop my mom from trying. My mom came from a less fortunate family that didn't have much growing up. She lost her father at 10-years old and my grandmother was left to take care of five kids on her own. My mother remembered that struggle and she was willing to do whatever was necessary to give her children better than what she had. My mother fought for a better future for her kids. She put her pride to the side and asked one of her co-workers to borrow 5k for the down payment. She went back to my dad with the money and that's when he realized she was determined to get the house. My mom paid her coworker back and she got the house she wanted.

Sacrifices were made and expenses were cut but my parents did what they had to do to give us the life they felt we deserved. As a little girl, I told my parents I wanted the house if they ever decided to sell it so they could move down south to enjoy their retirement. I'd lived in my family home since I was two years old and had a very strong attachment to it. So, when my dad said he had to let the house go, I asked him to refinance and let me live there and take over the mortgage! He was able to get the house refinanced due to the hardship of losing a spouse which made the mortgage affordable for me to move in and take over. My mom loved that house so I wasn't going to lose it without fighting to keep it first.

After I moved in, there were times when I wasn't able to feed my children or pay the utilities during the winter months, because I was only able to pay the mortgage since I received no financial assistance from my children's father. But I was determined to hold on to my family home any way that I could. Giving up on the house felt like I was giving up on my mother so throughout the years, I fought and I fought to keep it. Whenever I came up short on funds, my dad was always there doing what he could do to help.

In life, you truly have to fight for what's important to you and the life you desire to have. As years went on, life started to get better for my family and me. I'll never forget the day my dad looked at me and said "Thank you for having the strength to fight for our family home when no one else did!" When my mom passed away, he was broken by grief. Letting the house go was an emotional decision at the time. We can't allow our emotions to dictate our actions. It's never easy to fight for what's important to you but the courage, strength, and resilience you gain from that battle makes it all worthwhile. Having the opportunity to raise my children in my family home is a true blessing. I tell them stories and memories of their grandmother which is priceless.

Sometimes, while in the middle of the struggle, we believe that we are losing. But while fighting, we actually experience hidden wins, those victories that you can't see at the moment but they are there. You only recognize them later when you are able to stand back and assess your journey. It is then when you finally realize the gains you've experienced.

We don't always see our hidden victories but that is why it is so important to have a positive mindset instead of a negative one. Although I faced a job loss during the pandemic, I also experienced a **WINdemic** (even though I didn't realize it at first)! I mentioned to one of my friends that I wanted to fix up my basement a little at a time because it was too expensive to renovate all at once. Then one day, I came downstairs and my basement was flooded from a pipe that burst. My initial thought was, "Right now is not a good time for this to be happening." But then, I remembered how God is intentional.

With my home insurance settlement, the basement was completely gutted and remodeled. Thousands of dollars were spent to replace everything in my basement, yet it was money that didn't come from my bank account. With the money left over from the renovation, I was able to replace all the appliances in my kitchen and bathrooms. And by the time everything was completed, I honestly had a new home. God truly works all things for the good! In every aspect of my life, I was **Winning!** From publishing two best-selling books, becoming debt free, restoring my credit back to excellent, running two marathons, and my house being remodeled; I even got a chance to travel to Cuba and Costa Rica earlier in the year before the pandemic. I truly experienced a **WINdemic!**

Unleashing my greatness and fighting for my potential, no matter what obstacles I faced, caused me to have a breakout of nothing but Wins. I have been winning for some time now and every year gets better and better. You have to keep going even when everything around you makes you feel like you should stop! When life happens, that's when you have to show up for yourself even more. You have to envision yourself winning. You must ask yourself in the moments of doubt, uncertainty, fear, and hardships, "Is my future worth fighting for? Is fighting for my full potential worth fighting for?" The answer to those questions is, "Yes!" because you are worth fighting for!

The 2020 President Election was a historical moment for America and broke the record for how many people voted in a single election. Out of 239.2 million eligible voters, this year's 66 percent voter turnout rate tops anything the US ever experienced in the last century. Witnessing the first Black President eleven years ago and now experiencing the election of the first Black Woman Vice-President of the United States is truly incredible. Kamala D. Harris had a vision to one day become the President of the United States as a little girl and even at the age of 56, she never stopped fighting for her Full Potential. Being the first Black Woman elected as Vice-President is still one heck of an achievement, a victory that she worked for and a dream she was willing to fight for. Although she didn't become the President of the United States, she is one step closer to her dream and she made history!

When other people make their dreams a reality, it should also give you hope in knowing that your dream is possible as well. When you stop fighting for your full potential that's when you miss the opportunity to make your dreams a reality. Witnessing someone achieve what others once thought was impossible is life-changing and impactful. Their achievements can instill hope and encourage you to keep working towards your dreams. When you fight for your full potential you produce a greatness that spreads in the world. By fulfilling her potential, Kamala Harris just opened the door for other aspiring females. Just a century ago, women didn't have the right to vote and now we have a woman as VP. When you are willing to do the work, you will see the results from what you put in. I believe the 2020 Election and its historic victory will cause a **WINdemic** across the entire globe.

America has experienced a very rough and heartbreaking year with the loss of jobs and loved ones. But I believe even in the midst of this pandemic, we can still fight, hope, heal and believe that change will come and America will become better than ever.

I don't believe anyone can live up to their full potential without a Fight! Life will always bring forth challenges, obstacles, and hardships, yet those elements of life are what we must fight through! We have to fight through the naysayers, the odds set against us, our negative thoughts, our fears, our doubts, and any unfortunate circumstances that take place. Fighting for your potential will always be an ongoing battle because life will continue to happen. But you have to stay the course and be willing to take action!

I don't believe there is one human being on this earth who doesn't have greatness on the inside of them. And the difference between someone who lives in their greatness and someone who doesn't is the choice to fight for one's own potential. Fight so you can unleash the greatness that's on the inside of you. Ask yourself, "What are you willing to fight for?"

How many times have you found yourself moving in the right direction and everything was going well but then an unfortunate event took place that felt like someone just punched you in the gut? It caught you off-guard and you may have even lost your breath in that moment. But that's when you gather yourself, take a moment to reflect, and then refocus on your goals. Fighting for your full potential won't be an easy task but it will be a tough, ongoing, and rewarding one.

I am now at a place in my life where I would never take the easier route if the harder route will make me better. Fighting for your Full Potential is about wanting to be better than who you were yesterday! You are **the only one** responsible for living up to your full potential and your own Happiness. Someone's else's standard for you should never be higher than the standard you set for yourself. Don't get in the habit of always trying to prove others wrong but instead, get in the habit of always proving yourself right! Fighting for your Full Potential will cause you to develop that, "I Am. I Can. And I Will!" mindset! And you must refuse to let anything or anyone get in the way of what you told yourself you are going to do!

You can't choose a future for yourself that you aren't willing to fight for. We have to be willing to put the same amount of energy into ourselves that we choose to put into unhealthy relationships, toxic relationships, unbalanced relationships, or any other areas of life that don't make us better. My life changed drastically when I made a decision to work on myself inside and out. We have to want more for ourselves and do whatever is necessary to choose to fight for it! If you're not willing to fight for your full potential then you must be satisfied with having less or having a mediocre life. But you deserve more than mediocre! You can't keep allowing the world to bully you, pushing you around and telling you what you can and cannot do! At some point you are going to have to stand up and **FIGHT!** You can't back down and lay down any longer than what you already have. Enough is Enough! I told myself years ago that I was no longer going to keep accepting what the world was offering me but instead I was going to take what I wanted! Now is the time more than ever before that you need to start showing up for yourself.

Fighting for your full potential releases your greatness because it causes you to reveal certain characteristics about yourself you didn't know you had. As you learn more and more about yourself, that gives you the courage and confidence needed to go after your dreams. Fighting for your full potential holds you accountable and always allows you to be in control of your destiny. You have the power and the ability to choose your future. Fighting for your potential causes you to dig deep down in DEPTHS of who you are so you can discover what you are truly made of.

When you fight for your full potential and unleash your greatness, you make it possible for the next person to do the same. You never know who's watching you and counting on you from afar. You never know how your actions will affect the next person. You have to keep pushing, you have to keep fighting because someone's life does depend on it. Your dreams are Necessary!

Reflect & Refocus Key Points:

- Never allow your emotions to dictate your actions
- Never take the easier route if the harder route will make you better
- You owe it to yourself to show up and show out for yourself always
- Only you have the power to UNLEASH the Greatness that's on the inside of you
- Living up to your Full Potential and your Happiness is your Responsibility
- Someone else's standard for you should never be higher than the one you set for yourself.
- Don't make a habit of trying to prove everyone wrong but instead make a habit of proving yourself right!
- If you want to change your life in a Big Way, then you need to make some Big Changes!
- You have the power and the ability to choose your Future.

Fighting for your own potential will truly Unleash the Greatness that God has placed inside you. You owe it to yourself to become everything you've ever dreamed of becoming. Understand that nothing is more important than working on you! Focusing on me and my self-development has turned me into an A.G.C. (**AMBITIOUS GOAL CRUSHER**)

If there is a Dream on the inside of you but you need help accomplishing that dream, then contact me at JeniseMcNair@gmail.com to receive information about my Online Course **"Against All Odds; You Still Win!"** This online course is set up to help individuals leverage their setbacks while fearlessly going after the dreams they once thought were too hard or impossible. I strategically teach individuals how to Win in every aspect of their life.

Whether you have small or big goals ahead of you, there's power in the pursuit. Self-development is the foundation of who you are and your success! You are worth Fighting for your Full Potential and Unleashing the Greatness within you! There's always room for growth and improvement. I know working on yourself can be a very difficult and challenging task but that's why you have to be willing to fight for a better you! As you grow so does your vision. The only regret we should have in life is that we chose not to fight for our own potential or we didn't get a chance to see what our Greatness can produce. What do you have to lose, other than the opportunity of knowing just how great you are? When you fight for your full potential, you gain confidence to fearlessly go after the life you feel you deserve.

The world will try to throw everything your way to stop you from unleashing your greatness but don't ever let it stop you from pushing ahead. You can't want a future for yourself that you aren't willing to fight for! Remember, when you fight for your full potential, that's when you make the impossible possible!

Fighting for your Full Potential will be one of the toughest fights of your life but also the most rewarding! Don't ever back down from anything because **YOU ARE WORTH THE FIGHT!**

About the Author

Jenise is an Entrepreneur, Best-Selling Author, Certified Life Coach, and Motivational Speaker who is determined to get the best out of life, despite obstacles that may arise. Jenise has been featured on several news outlets including ABC, NBC, CBS, and FOX. Jenise overcame so many disappointments and hardships that tried to prevent her from unleashing her Greatness Within. After years of feeling like she was losing in life, she recognized that she would only be able to live up to her Full Potential if she was willing to fight for it. Developing a Winning mindset taught Jenise how to leverage her setbacks so she can take the lead and Win! Jenise is now a seven-time Marathoner who understands if you really want something in life, you have to be willing to go get it!

Jenise transformed her life by only focusing on her Self-Development and trying to become the Greatest Version of herself. Jenise is truly a lover of people and a natural motivator who encourages and inspires others to go after their dreams, despite obstacles that try to get in the way. Jenise is passionate about helping others walk in their personal truths, take ownership over their Happiness, and truly love themselves within. As a Mindset Coach, Jenise believes when you mentally challenge yourself and choose to be better than who you were yesterday, nothing can stop you from getting the best out of life.

Jenise lives in Largo, Maryland and is the mother of three amazing children, Jelani, Jaylah, and Jordyn. She learned how to overcome adversity by developing mental fortitude and beating all the odds set to prevent her growth as a woman and mother. She believes your circumstances in life are only permanent when you choose to accept them as defeat. She believes you are only as Great as you think you are, So, don't just think you're Great, know you're Great!

www.ingramcontent.com/pod-product-compliance
Lightning Source LLC
LaVergne TN
LVHW021405080426
835508LV00020B/2473

Your inner girl is calling.
Listen – She wants to
Explore, Experience and Live.
~Sunnie Givens